NOBODY

Perseverance Of A Sharecropper's Son

A Life, from
"...Hey, Water Boy!"
To a Master's Degree and This Beyond!

JOSEPH LEWIS JOHNSON

PRESS

Nobody
Perseverance of a Sharecropper's Son
by Joseph Lewis Johnson

Printed in the United States of America

ISBN 9781498406215

www.xulonpress.com

Dedicated to…
My savior God and Christ
My enslaved & entrapped ancestors
My Mother Lizzie Josephine, a Saint
My precious & remarkable wife Jean, love of my life…
My wonderful daughter Joan Niccole, her husband Justin
and their first Child (my 1st grandchild),
"Aubrey Jean!"
My courageous son, Joseph Marshall!

Those who enlightened me

I would like to also acknowledge...

My uncle JD Fountain; my oldest living brothers, Sam and Sim; and my only sister, Lueretha, and cousins Barbra Tucker and Derrick Anderson for their insight into our family's early years.

Dr. Thomas Baldwin Jones, for his uncanny love of teaching hundreds of non-traditional and troubled young boys, girls and adults, like myself, the art of phonics.

My father in-law, John Rustad, for his meticulous demand for detail.

Editors Mary Jo Brzezinski and Don Brosius.

Photo Enhancement Kendra Niederkorn.

And last, but certainly not least, Mr. Robert (*Say it ain't so, Joe!*) Weirauch, my beloved friend, who's been a fountain of inspiration with words of wisdom, encouragement and his continuous generosity to me and my family.

TABLE OF CONTENTS

Anchor Curve, Mississippi

MY ORIGIN AND FAITH

Once I stopped and reflected for a brief moment on how much God had to love me to create me in His own Omnipotent image! And give me the ability to reproduce biologically what I am, a human being! And the offspring that I reproduce, I will love them unconditionally.

Therefore the compelling question becomes....?

Should I dare to believe that "Adam," my first forefather, was formed from the dust of the ground, in the image of God, in a remote part of His enormous universe, the Garden of Eden? "*And the breath of life was breathed into his nostrils by God; and man became a living soul...*" "*Adam.*" Or that I, too, was created in the likeness of my heavenly Father as was Adam; so should there be any doubts that He has the same unconditional love for me?

To further understand God as my creator, first I needed to understand that He self-exists, whereas I am a created being of Him. His creations also include all living kinds of plants and animals. Therefore, when I understood that

I am a human being formed by my Creator, I then realized that I am also ultimately accountable to Him! Made "vital" that I had no choice but to pursue Christ's likeness in all aspects of my life so I would be able to encourage that same accountability in my family and others. And I must put complete trust in Him that He will provide for all of His creations.

As a believer, I know that no matter who I am or where I was born, I am incredibly important to God. I am not only body and soul, but a spiritual being with intelligence, perception, and the ability to determine my own destiny within His will. Therefore, I am accountable and responsible to God for all that He has given me.

I should never be pleased to live on a level of existence lower or higher than what God has called me to be and equipped me for. And any true success in life does not come from the sins behind the quick-fix schemes promoted by sinful acts. If this were not so, why would our Savior and Creator's son, Jesus Christ, have to die? To find the way to redemption, I had to separate myself from this world system's earthly lies. I can do this only with strong values and a faithful Helper through God to reject greed, pride and their amenities (sins). I am so thankful that I needed to be accountable to my Creator.

VALIDATION

To validate my autobiography, I have worked with genealogists from the Department of Archives and Records Services Division, Jackson, Mississippi; researchers specializing in Mississippi genealogy and history; legal records from the United States Census dating back to the 1800s; ancestors' travel records and authentications; and finally, the enlightenment of my ancestral history, traditions and heritage, as well as my personal memories, which were strengthened by an uncle, my oldest brothers, my sister and cousins.

All Bible verses in this autobiography are from the New King James, Spirit – Filled Life Student Bible, Growing in the Power of the Word – 1995 (Nelson Bibles – A Division of Thomas Nelson Publishers Since 1789).

FOREWORD

Over 66 years, my travels have taken me...

➢ From the steamy cotton fields of the Mississippi Delta, Anchor Curve...

➢ To the rough and tumble streets of Chicago, Illinois...

➢ To my days of *"Make love not war!"* in the drug infested streets of Oakland, California...

➢ To two Mississippi Junior Colleges...

➢ To a Bachelor of Science Degree from Aurora College (now Aurora University) in Aurora, Illinois...

➢ To working as a Youth Supervisor and Counselor in a Juvenile Corrections Center, in St. Charles, Illinois...

➢ To Madison, Wisconsin, (a University town that seems always to be in some kind of turmoil) Program Director at Project Bootstrap, an after-school program, and undergrad student...

➢ To Wausau, Wisconsin, our home for 14 years; and was once the whitest Congressional District in the United States...

➢ To Bridgewater, MA, the place my remarkable wife, Jean, and I now call home!

Tipping Point!

Complicated by both real and imaginary adversities and a general lack of respect for others and myself, I was headed for trouble. My propensity for living a life-style of self-indulgence was slowly but surely destroying the person I wanted to be from my days in Oakland through the times I lived in Aurora. Gradually, I began to realize that I was headed down the road to nowhere and something needed to change! I can recall exactly when that change began to take place: a week after my 43rd birthday, November 17, 1990, Aurora, Illinois! I began to seek out answers. Was I going to continue to risk a lifetime of happiness with my wife and kids under God and Christ's control for a few minutes of sinful pleasure here and there according to this world's system? *I heard this subtle but mysterious voice out of nowhere that said to me "Move to Madison!"* I found God. Or maybe God found me! Since that time, my life changed for the better in ways I couldn't possibly have achieved on my own. However, like most repenting sinners there is always room for improvement!

Therefore, I'm not writing this autobiography to harm anyone's feelings, integrity, sensibility or beliefs. I just want to explain how God's Truth, Jesus Christ, has helped me transform from just another "Nobody" to a productive somebody who became a caring husband, parent and a valued member of society!

I believe that an individual's integrity can only be blemished through his/her thoughtless, selfish acts, not by the acts of others. I realized that I was damaging my integrity by not adhering to a code of positive values,

God's Commandments. These values taught me that my negative acts will invariably come back to haunt me, and like sins, they must be purged to gain forgiveness and true happiness. But remember, God's word said that I'm accountable for my own sins at judgment day, not the sins of another.

It is my sincere hope that the events of my early life might aid in helping others improve and enrich their lives. My quest is to substantiate fact from fiction, uttered or printed by the storytellers among my ancestors.

As a descendant of uneducated slaves and share-croppers, to earning a Master's Degree and becoming a faithful Servant of an "agape love" (a state of astonishment and wonder), I've finally come to terms with my journey. As an at-risk child and a nontraditional student, I was faced with a choice – give into what most, at one time, believed me to be: *Nobody – just another insignificant person of no authority or position,* or fight back! I chose the latter!

My professional career consisted of thirty-five-plus years of working with at-risk, latchkey and other nontraditional elementary, middle and high school students. These students were, for the most part, deemed "Nobodies," such as me. This, coupled with the primitive school systems I attended as a child, initially, I thought, was all I had to work with.

Don't misunderstand me. Working in Juvenile Corrections, Residential Treatment and as an academic entrepreneur has been a rewarding privilege. I have strived toward having my work convey the values and hope that this autobiography is intended to extend. With God's leadership, I will continue to support the things I believe nontraditional families and their children need to have in order to remove the stigma of ignorance and mediocrity from their lives. These are: faith; hope; support; education; and most importantly, Love!

Many of today's pre, current and post-adolescents (regardless of race or gender) are clearly the victims of illiteracy. The root causes of this situation likely date back to centuries of primitive day-to-day existence, followed by the horrors of slavery, followed by an empty freedom often caused by the lack of an adequate education. In most cases, this led to a life of "pseudo-slavery," which included menial jobs such as sharecropping, migrant working, housekeeping, etc. The sober consequences of this condition frequently trickled down into habitual truancy for generation upon generation of unfortunate, innocent children, who had little hope for the future.

For many, this resulted in a predictable life of broken spirits, relationships, marriages and homes filled with chaos and adversity. And little has changed over the years.

Abbreviated School Years

The truancy epidemic! Unfortunately for many children, today's increase in the *truancy epidemic* at the elementary school level can lead to nowhere but disaster for the children–and for society as a whole! It is wreaking havoc on our children's education today, as it has done for decades! This ugly backlash continues to render many children statistically unemployable by the time they become young adults–except in manual laborers such as the Mississippi cotton fields! These adolescents and undereducated adults (especially males) are now facing disastrous lives of desolation in crime-infested communities, without the faintest hopes or dreams of pulling themselves out of this condition–except perhaps in some, to be named *sports arena, recording studio, or farfetched movie set!*

In 1878, the South was forced by the federal government to create public school systems to help educate freed slaves, as well as any poor white children who had only a passing acquaintance with formal education. However, it is no coincidence that in 1918, Mississippi became the *last State in America* to enact the Compulsory Education law, which required public school children to attend classes for a given number of hours each week and a given number of days each year; or until a certain age, typically 16 or 18.

However, state and school officials in our rural Mississippi village tended to look the other way when children, who were expected to attend school, were instead working in the cotton fields! This meant that the school years for rural Mississippi sharecroppers' adolescents like me were unfortunately much shorter than the school years of my peers of the affluent black land owners and those living in northern states where Compulsory Education Laws were more strictly enforced.

Sharecroppers' children were needed at three different times during the school year: After "Spring Cultivation and planting," which included hoeing or chopping to thin out the cotton to keep it from suffocating; "Weeding" (mid–April through June) to also prevent the cotton plants from suffocating; and the "Fall Harvest" (cotton picking) in late October, November and into December. We were held out of school for that specific purpose!

My older brothers and sister were only allowed to attend school during off season, due to the fact that children were needed in the fields for both the planting and harvesting seasons. None of the sharecroppers' kids were able to successfully complete high school, in part because of the practice of "abbreviated school years." Though this policy wasn't necessarily legal, it was tolerated with a wink and a nod! This sort of mandatory child labor was common in our village for many years. Believe it or not, it's still tolerated in some areas today.

In my case, these abbreviated school years were in play until 1966, my sophomore year in Montgomery High School, Louise, Mississippi. For my two younger brothers and me, as well as many other local children, all of that would eventually change, but not soon enough to affect our personal development. And years later, those factors still plague most former children of sharecroppers today, including me!

Personal and Ancestral Journeys

Let me share with you the significant characteristics that eventually helped me to define my life through perseverance and faith in God. It's how I viewed life from the aspect of a child living with several brothers and a sister in a single parent home. Growing up in Anchor Curve, we spoke a dialect now dubbed Black English Vernacular (BEV) comprised of odd and often abbreviated words and incomplete sentences. For example, in our family's case, if the big boss wanted to know why my sister was absent from the field, my mother might explain: *my daughter sick (which indicates a current sickness of short-term duration). My daughter she is sick (indicates longer term duration for illness).* This, coupled with our relatively primitive local education system, might have led me into a life of semi-illiteracy and poverty...but I wasn't about to let that happen!

Through my ancestors' journeys, their enslavement eventually evolved into the scheme of sharecropping, a system of free or very cheap labor! This negatively impacted the lives of thousands of people, mostly black but other ethnicities as well. Sharecropping was created for the sole purpose of generating and maintaining a *way of life that consisted* of continuum of free to cheap labor in the Mississippi Delta, from the middle 1800s to the late 1900s, leaving generations of sharecroppers uneducated and unemployable outside of those cotton fields!

Belief in a Supernatural Being is part of what my 18th-century African enslaved ancestors brought with them to America. And for many, these beliefs are still in place today. Through oral histories and historians' documents, I've learned of their long, difficult, terrifying voyages, jammed into the stench filled holds of countless slave ships for six months thanks to Dr. Henry Louis Gates Jr. documentary <u>Many Rivers to Cross</u>, Second Great Middle Passage March (SGMPM). Those who survived passed these stories on from generation to generation.

But who actually were my ancestors? Where did they come from? When did they get here? What were their lives like before captivity? And how do these answers affect my life and possibly impact yours?

Before I decided to excavate my ancestral past, all I really knew with certainty was that I was a sharecropper's son who grew up in what we called the Big House in Anchor Curve, Mississippi, and earlier it was also known as the "Craig Community," four miles southeast of the small town of Louise, Mississippi. Before I could do that, however, I felt I needed a deeper understanding of the essence of storytelling. In an effort to absorb some of these concepts, I read all or parts of several relevant books and biographies, including: the Biblical Books of Job and Jeremiah; Barack Obama's <u>Dreams from My Father</u>; Sidney Poitier's <u>The Measure of a Man</u>; Lalita Tademy <u>Caine River;</u> plus others.

For me it was motivation, or *fire in my belly!* This is painfully apparent, for example, in the biblical Book of Job; it speaks of sins and being punished, where Job said, "I am not sorry enough for some wickedness"! For thousands of years, the biblical Books of Job and Jeremiah, asked readers to answer the same question: WHY? It is my hope that my story can help answer someone's "WHY?"

The "Backstory"...No Fairytale!

MY life at Anchor Curve was indeed harsh and demanding and left little time for play. I had often wondered how young children in other parts of the world spent their days. Were they required to work in fields? Or were their lives filled with running and playing like the white and affluent black children in our surrounding communities? Or how about life in Chicago, where my uncles, older brothers, and cousins lived? Since there were no cotton, soybean, or corn fields in the city, were my cousins required to work in factories? Did they have enough time to study hard yet play games? Did they have electricity, television, telephones, or indoor plumbing?

Hot and cold running water? Bathrooms instead of out-houses? We certainly didn't!

What a contrast from the life I lived in the Mississippi Delta. The northern kids seemed to live a fairytale existence. On the other hand, as a sharecropper's son my life consisted of ancient, almost barbaric living and working conditions that began at sunup and ended at sundown, just like my mom and her sisters, brothers, and our ancestors.

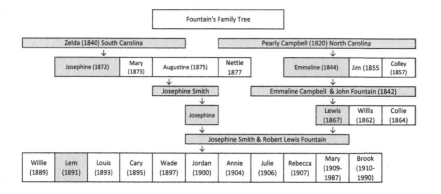

Chapter 1

THE BEGINNING

1 Timothy 6:1: "Let as many bond slaves as are under the yoke of their own master worthy of all honor, so that the name of God and His doctrine may not be blasphemed…"

Authentication (Storytellers Lore)!

I'm not a genealogist, nor did I initially wish to become one but was thoroughly hooked when I began researching my family history. Even to the point of not watching the games I so profoundly loved on television (football and basketball) or playing tennis. I found myself being drawn to dig deeper into my ancestors' lives, which I had intentionally avoided as a teen and younger man. I was amazed that I was able to track my ancestors back to the early 1800s. When I first started my research, it seemed insurmountable. After all, rich dandies' livestock were better documented than their slaves!

With the invention of the cotton gin in 1793 by Eli Whitney, the southern states could produce more cotton and needed more hands to work the cotton fields, making my ancestors and many other slaves a commodity. Professor Henry Louis Gates Jr. **Many Rivers to Cross** documentary explained how many of my ancestors ended up in the Mississippi Delta as part of the Second Great Middle Passage March (SGMPM). It took place around 1790 and lasted nearly ninety years, stretching across five states from Georgia to Texas. With Mississippi centrally located within those five states and its rich soil and proximity to the huge tow-boats and barges that plied the mighty Mississippi and Yazoo rivers, the Delta was the heart of America's cotton belt until the late 20th Century. This placed some of my ancestors at the slave markets in Vicksburg and Natchez, Mississippi.

I had always tried to avoid recalling my ancestors' past outside that of Mom and my grandparents being share-croppers. We lived discrimination on a daily basis, so I had no desire to add to that pressure by delving into what my ancestors had to endure as young enslaved children, which evolved into the early sharecropping regime in the Mississippi Delta. So I guess you can say that the lore of their past was kept locked away in a secured chamber of my heart—until my return to complete graduate school forced me to relive that period in history that I so badly wanted to leave in the past.

For my final graduate school requirement, I chose to write a Thesis Project about truancy at the elementary school levels. In my initial writing about truancy, I had incorporated my encounters with it as a sharecropper's son growing up in the Delta cotton fields in the 1950s and

60s. To validate how I experienced truancy by a means of forced abbreviated school days, I had to remember all past lore of the storytellers. The lore told of a legacy of forced illiteracy dating back approximately one hundred and fifty years. What a harsh reality it was to summon up more than fifteen decades of denied educational opportunities and how my future was trying to be shaped by my ancestors!

In the preliminary stage of editing my Theses Project with my advisor, Dr. Marty Loy of the University of Wisconsin Stevens Point, he stopped me and suggested that I write an autobiography instead because it would be a "better read" than just another abstract document on truancy; due to my perseverance through those abbreviated school years. He believed this was something that my family and other families could read for inspiration to benefit their children's academic situations.

It was unpleasant and heart-wrenching to learn that my ancestors were forced to come to this country physically and materially naked, debarked of their traditions. But it was rewarding to know that their souls and spirit were one of great faith, filled with rich cultural contributions, which they would eventually pass on to several generations, to my Mom, who passed it on to my generation. Their many unique gifts and artistic talents contributed substantially to mine and civilization's growth and development on the North American continent.

Much of American Delta agriculture was built upon the backs of slave labor as described by Ira Berlin in his book *The Making of African America,* and Dr. Henry Louis Gates Jr. Documentary "**African American, Many Rivers to Cross**."

To further understand enslavement and learn where my bloodlines started, I had to endure the recall of how slavery and its unpleasant byproducts affected them and forced their submission to its cruelty. For instance, if slavery were a tree, then one byproduct of that tree could be the paper that this autobiography is written on! My research revealed that paper is made by diluting a suspension of wood fibers in water, which is drained through a screen, so that a mat of randomly interwoven fibers is laid down.

Slavery diluted and tried to destroy the value and customs of my ancestors as well as the millions of Africa's brothers and sisters in Christ in the SGMPM, implying that they were less than human. Making their major byproduct free labor! So my next heart-wrenching question was, why slave ownership automatically entitled the slave owner to dominate my family and many others in order to obtain free labor? Did simply possessing a forced piece of paper claiming ownership of them make it legal, right, or Godly? If so, then the trees used for papermaking are specifically grown and harvested for that purpose, so history is telling me that my ancestors and those involved in the SGMPM were born for a specific purpose, to be free laborers for the rich!

My beloved ancestors along with countless others were also put through a "debarking" process that removed their names and individualities in an attempt to get rid of their family traditions and values, and then given their masters' last names (in many cases) and persona. They couldn't even get married without their owners' permission and pursuing an education was totally forbidden.

Surviving, not fear, became my great, great, great, and great, great grandparents' main focus, because they were living in a strange land and knew very little of its spoken language. Where were they to go? They had to depend on their masters for survival. Their masters' strategic plan was to keep them uneducated to the written linguistic to ensure power and control to prevent emancipation. Though their emancipation was withheld from them for many decades, it did finally come in the wake of my generation. Finally, my great, great, great grandparents, great, great grandparents, great grandparents, grandparents and mother had a strategic plan more powerful than their masters. Because their strategic plan involved God and Christ as their savior, they never gave up HOPE of being free individuals, just as their fore parents did in the old country (Africa). Even if it meant waiting until they were called home to be with God. Their survival skills of faith and perseverance had been passed through four generations to me, the storyteller, so I could pass it on to future generations.

This whole scenario of slavery, which would eventually evolve into a sharecropping scheme in the early-to-mid-1900s, was mind boggling and downright painful for me to study and comprehend. It's not like they taught this to us as children or through educational history in my all black school. These American "dandies" went to all the trouble to travel thousands of miles by sea to a faraway unfamiliar country to find free or other enslaved and captured children of God, then enslave them and take them on a dangerous voyage of ten or more months to a strange country, America. Then they beat them into submission, attempting to destroy any and all of their customs for the sole purpose of retaining a "Gentile" way of life. UNBELIEVABLE! How could these men even call themselves Christians and stoop to such a superior form of cruelty for free labor and greed of the worst kind? Unaccustomed to their captive ways of life and the brutality they had to endure during their extensive journey in the bottom of that ship, I can envision just how easy it was to forcefully mold the majority of them into people of obedience, to perform their masters' grueling, backbreaking labor from sunup to sundown without compensation. After, they were paraded on a stage for sale to the highest bidder at slave auctions from Natchez and Vicksburg, Mississippi and the East Coast shoreline!

So I asked myself, "Who attends a slave auction?" I found my answer in Dr. Theophilus Kramer's account of a slave auction, from The Slave-auction on openlibrary.com. That's right, a real slave auction, where my ancestors and possibly some of yours were bought and sold like livestock.

In 1859, Dr. Kramer wrote his account of a slave auction. He stated that his motive for writing about slave auctions was not a political one. He was plainly trying to answer the question: "Can slavery and Christianity coexist?" Dr. Kramer's writings provided a detailed picture of what he saw with his own eyes. While residing and writing in some of the slave states for more than ten years, Kramer wondered, "how a white Christian can treat a person of color like an animal? Who gave permission for white Christians to sell his black, yellow or brown brothers, sisters and even children at a public auction for money?" While writing about them, Dr. Kramer had personal concerns and ill feelings against the owners of slaves in the Slave States of the Union but was particularly adverse to the Institution of slavery itself!

As a believer in God and Christ, I certainly understand and agree with Dr. Kramer that any individual who could be even remotely involved in the selling of human beings for any reason could hardly call themselves Christians! True Christians are to heed the wicked transgressions of this world that thrives on its own selfish greed! That those who do call themselves Christians but carry on evil deeds and lawless acts without redemption comes Judgment Day, *(paraphrase)* He (Jesus Christ) would say to them, "away with you for I never knew you" (Mt 7: 23.) I am obligated to speak out against the wrongdoing of any person, regardless of their relationship to me, race, creed, color or national origin. Not speaking out only takes us back to barbarianism and diminishes the growth of free civilization.

As shown in the following description of a slave auction "call," the slave auctioneer calls to the assemblage: "They were born as slaves, through the iniquity of men. They are redeemed to be free, through Jesus Christ," intones the auctioneer. I argue we all were born as slaves to sin and to be redeemed by Christ for our sinful nature, but not to be slaves for man's selfish greed!

Quite naturally I can't speak to this firsthand or personally, but once again from Dr. Kramer's account and the lore of ancestors, I became the storyteller of what my Great, Great, Great Grandfather John Fountain must have had to endure at a young age in a Vicksburg, Mississippi, slave auction. The headlines leading up to that day's auction were advertising—along with newspapers, tacked-up posters, hand-outs, and word-of-mouth—gave the times and dates of slaves to be sold at the Broad Hall on Market Street, Vicksburg, Mississippi.

Slave Poster

These auctions attracted the rich and not-so-rich customers, both male and female, and surprisingly, not all of them were Caucasian! Mother Africa's strongest, possibly some were my ancestors, who I will never know about; young and old males and females; single and married; some children were sold to the highest bidders for cheap laborers and propagators for future laborers. Now, from what I recalled from our family lore and historic reading, presumably, my Great, Great, Great Grandparents were called...to bondage.

What I read was beyond belief, the slave auction venues and the gala events that often surrounded them seemed imaginary! The atmosphere was described as quite stylish, with beautiful paintings adorning the walls, with elegant furnishings to admire and enjoy. As richly dressed, often overweight, dandies helped themselves to fine liquors and smoked their Havana cigars while soaking up their lavish surroundings. Alongside splendidly dressed ladies *(yes, ladies!)* dressed in their finest French silk and satin gowns and glittering precious jewels. Even the display of chivalry was present as they bounced up from their seats to politely offer their chairs to their feminine counterparts. When the doors opened, a large number of Mother Africa's strongest and finest entered the hall, which encompassed some of my ancestors, like herds of cattle going to market. Instead, it was actually a gathering for the sale of human flesh cunningly disguised as a social event!

I can visualize my ancestors and others of that assemblage disagreeable and in great pain as they were that first day's stockpile of "merchandise." Their skin colors differed. Some of them were as black as ebony, the native Africans. Some brown and some yellow-toned from being the byproduct of their captives and first masters. As they marched onto the stage in front of the elegantly dressed audience, most knew their lives would never be the same. Not a one of them dared to raise their head or an eye to look at their soon-to-be masters.

Imagine the anguish these young and old souls alike must have felt as they were being paraded across a stage to be viewed for sale like livestock? I asked myself how I would have felt in that situation. Or think of the babies in their mothers' arms and ask yourself this: could those babies feel their mothers' misery? I think so, even if they would never remember that instant of sorrow. I'll never forget reading the stories or listening to lore that told of their deep distress. I imagined the look on the faces of all those unfortunate little children standing near or being held by their mothers in that moment in time, on that auction stage.

Slave cabins, or quarters, and later sharecropper housing, provided one of the few places where our ancestors could be more or less free from constant supervision by their overseers. There they created a vibrant social and cultural life beyond the reach of their masters. No rational person would wish to be a slave; even though my ancestors were and their lives were restricted in many significant ways, they sought to make the best of their circumstances. Eventually most of them succeeded, which is a testimony to the endurance of the human spirit through God and Christ.

My hope or objective remains to ensure that my bloodline and group identity do not determine my children's destiny. Today, many white Americans can look back at how far they have come in this country. On the other hand, my ancestors and their descendants, especially my generation (as well as many other minority races), still look at how far we have to go to be free and get a fair share of the American dream. Both narratives have some validity, but blacks and other minorities still have more to accomplish, even with the election of our first black President, Barack Obama.

A Plea for Togetherness… In Lieu of Freedom

During my pre-adolescence I spent most of my time with Grandma Retta, listening to the old stories passed down by family members. These stores encompass their supplication of faith for togetherness, customs, tradition, and how important family values were in lieu of their freedom. I also consulted with other family members as storytellers: Uncle JD Fountain, the youngest and only living child of Lem and Retta Fountain; my oldest living brothers, Sam and Sim; and my only sister, Lueretha. After I learned of the hardship that my ancestors had to endure in order for our family to remain united together, I was left with no other choice but to include their suffering as a part of my perseverance memoirs. However, at that time I didn't know of the horrific things that they had to accept, along with giving up all hope of freedom for family unity. I have always had a hard time accepting social injustice, whether in real life, on television, movies, even in sporting events. For that reason, I never read the books nor wished to see the television series <u>Roots</u> by Alex Haley, or <u>Mississippi Burning</u> by Alan Parker, because I would get infuriated if I did.

After I listened to an oral version of my Great, Great, Great Grandparents' time in captivity, and the circumstance surrounding what they endured in the Slave Market in Natchez and Vicksburg, I became inflamed and furious with anger until I could feel it burning into the pit of my soul. That's when I knew I had no choice but to write about their journey, as well.

From the data I collected, I was able to authenticate a clear depiction of four spirited and faithful slave girls, initially known as: Pearly, Zelda, Rachel, and Rebecca (including some folklores). Although they were born in North Carolina, South Carolina, Maryland, and Alabama, they all ended up in the Mississippi Delta; what a contrast! According to the 1870 United States Federal Census report, my Great, Great, Great Grandmother Pearly of North Carolina, born 1820, appeared as Pearly Campbell with three children, Emmaline (1844), Jim (1855) and Colley (1857). *Emmaline Campbell,* the oldest of three, would become my Great, Great, Grandmother by wedding John Fountain *born 1842 in Virginia.* They would have three children: Collie (1864), Willis (1862), and *Robert Lewis Fountain (January 1867);* the oldest would become my Great, Great Grandfather.

This bond of togetherness would be put to the test even before leaving the slave market in Vicksburg, Mississippi. John Fountain and Emmaline Campbell had somehow bonded before being forced to take the auction stage. Emmaline and her family had been sold to S.H. Whitworth and placed under the supervision of her master's overseer. (S. H. Whitworth had the land until it was deeded on February 2, 1876, according to the Humphreys County Deed Record Transcribed Book 5, page 281, to a Robert Craig and sons. Robert Craig then deeded the land to W. C. and R. E. Craig, 1/19/1884, the Humphreys County Deed Record Transcribed Book 6 page 7. Then to L. G. and L. J. Montgomery, then to the Federal Land Bank in New Orleans, and finally to Lawrence Macklin December 4, 1946, which is where my direct history started.)

This would leave behind John Fountain and his family. His adored Emmaline felt hopeless and thought that they would never be together after that day. As she was led away from the slave auction stage, John was waiting for his turn to be sold to the highest bidder. To Emmaline this was just another test of her faith, a faith that had been passed down through generations. She thought she would face a life without John. However, they never gave up on their hope and faith that God through Christ and the Holy Spirit would somehow reunite them.

Shortly after leaving the slave market, en route to Emmaline's new home in Green Hill Precinct plantation some 60 miles away, Great, Great, Great Grandmother and relatives continued to pray, weep, and beg Master Whitworth to return to the auction and buy John, as he was known to her. She promised they would be good slaves, stay and work his land, and never run away. Allegedly moved by this outcry of commitment, Master Whitworth stopped the wagon! And left his overseer in charge as he returned to the slave auction to find and bid for John. As Mr. Whitworth arrived back at the slave market, John was being auctioned off...

John's Call to Bondage...

I can still hear that call from my research! "My good friends," the auctioneer would say to the assembly, "John... a field hand... young. Ladies and gentlemen, this is a young-blood one of great capital worth! He is a great boy! A hand for almost everything! He also knows how to 'pray'! How much will you bid for him?" The bidding frenzy started at one thousand dollars by...

"Who is going to bid two thousand? Bidder # 14, One thousand dollars."

"Bidder 8, Twelve hundred dollars!"

"Bidder #14 says Twelve hundred and fifty dollars!"

"One thousand two hundred and fifty dollars! That's a fine bid, all right, but John is worth more – much more!"

"Do I hear thirteen hundred? Yes, the lady in the back row holding up the #18 says thirteen hundred!"

"Thirteen hundred? A bad number, ladies and gentlemen! Don't let John rest at thirteen hundred."

"Fourteen hundred and fifty dollars! Too small an amount for John! A strong, healthy, fine-looking, intelligent boy, Fourteen hundred and fifty dollars!"

"Gentlemen, John is worth more on my word! One thousand, four hundred and fifty... going! Fourteen hundred and fifty for the first... second... going?"

"Fourteen hundred and fifty dollars going! Going! Going! And last, gone! John is sold to you, sir. Please state your name..! Mr. Whitworth!"

Once Master Whitworth returned to the wagon train with John, he appeared to be a good master who would not sell the young couple. So from what I knew of them and their faith so far, I ask myself this question, were they being loyal servants? Or could the Bible verse 1 Timothy 6:1 be why they honor and respected their master, as they were true believers in God and Jesus Christ?

The remaining journey to Whitworth's plantation was one of challenging episodes of fighting off Mother Nature, defending the caravan from being ambushed by dangerous animals, "especially black panthers," known to be lurking along that treacherous, uninhabited wagon trail. Thick woods along many stretches of the trail prevented the travelers from seeing more than five feet beyond either side of the road. While the small settlements along the wagon trail seemed to be hundreds of miles apart, they were, in fact, only about fifteen to twenty miles apart. As the weary travelers passed through these woods, they had to trust in God and Christ to keep them safe. Many times their faith was tested, not unlike the Israelites in the wilderness. There was nothing left to do but put their trust and hope in their Creator.

Fighting the heat and humidity, Emmaline and the other girls were often forced to walk between the wagons when not riding. Blood sucking parasites, such as mosquitoes and horseflies, added to their misery, as they stepped around the manure left by horses, mules, and possibly other animals. Along with the men, young boys like John walked on both sides of the wagon train to fight off creatures and insects lurking in the dense undergrowth of scrub oak trees.

That situation became more pronounced and dangerous at the junction of Yazoo City and the primitive roads that ran through the Panther Creek Swamp area. Each night, the group had to find a safe place to encamp and sleep. This was not an easy job when approaching Panther Creek Swamp. The swamp was known to be the den of vicious black panthers, some of the most feared animals in that area, waiting to pounce upon the wary travelers or horses. Just thinking about the name Panther Creek Swamp must have filled the travelers with fear. Yet it had to be traversed. Even as a child, I feared that area and did not want to be out after dark, especially during mating season.

As they approached this dangerous swamp, Master Whitworth decided not to spend a night near this hazardous area, since they were no more than ten miles from his plantation. So he passed out kerosene lanterns and instructed wagon drivers to light their lanterns, armed himself with a shotgun, and kept the wagons moving. As morning broke, the weary travelers reached their final destination, the Whitworth family Plantation, Green Hill Precinct, Yazoo County.

Now the true test of their loyalty would be tried as they worked for decades on the same plantation. Even though plantation work was hard, their masters treated them decently compared to the dismal working conditions and what others had to endure on different plantations in the area. After being under the mastership of the Whitworth plantation supervision for two years, and having been good slaves, Emmaline and John promised that if they were allowed to marry, they would have children to help work his cotton fields, thus producing more crops. Emmaline and John worked and lived their entire life on that plantation while raising three children.

Of course, this is family folklore, but very interesting folklore! I find it very compelling that the "master" was shown in a positive light instead of the ever-present ogre of the south. I believe that most folklore has a basis in truth and enjoy this positive look at what was an awful time in history.

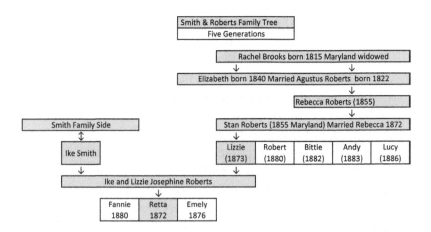

Chapter 2

THE FOLKLORE ENDS...

W e know that Robert Lewis Fountain, addressed by his middle name and the oldest son of John and Emmaline, would befriend Josephine Rebecca Smith, born 1872, also addressed by her middle name and the oldest daughter of Zelda, born 1840, and Samuel Smith, born 1810, of South Carolina. Lewis, age 19, and the 14-year-old Rebecca were allowed to marry on the 24th day of April 1886 at a cost of one hundred dollars! (Not that I consciously planned it, but I address both of my children by their middle names!)

Another generation that worked their entire lives on the same plantation even after the land ownership exchanged hands several more times.

Lewis and Rebecca were the first generation of freed slaves turned sharecroppers. Many generations of my family worked this land, with the longest stretch of ownership being under the Craig family and referred to as the Craig Community. Eventually, the area took on the name of Anchor Curve, as it remains to this day. The best we can tell, it became Anchor Curve during the ownership of Montgomery.

Lewis and Rebecca Fountain's Marriage License

According to my grandparents and mother, Lewis did not talk much about his parents and grandparents. However, they did talk about their legacy, faith in God and Christ, and how they were involved in the development of their community and church. They spoke about their love for their culture, their reasons for living, the importance of togetherness and family value. They also passed on their secret recipes for ethnic food preparations and the need to pass them on to future generations.

Great Grandfather Lewis Fountain was a sharecropper as well as carpenter. He used his skills to help build houses and their church, Big Mount Zion. Great Grandmother Rebecca Fountain was involved in the church as an usher. They were both regular attendees of Big Mount Zion. That's how important God was to them in keeping their family intact at any cost, even if it meant giving up their freedom per se and being enslaved their entire life; even after slavery had ended, sharecropping wasn't much different! They did not blame God for generations of hardships, or the slave traders and owners who touched our families at the slave market in Vicksburg, Mississippi; they were grateful to God and Christ for the events that made our family.

Even though my great grandparents were not academically educated, they were educated with God's wisdom. This wisdom enabled them to build a strong community that encompassed family togetherness, homes, and churches. They raised nine children, with Lem Fountain being the second oldest, born 1891: my grandfather. Without having a real school to attend, they learned by listening, doing, and watching. The Holy Bible was the only reading material they typically were allowed to have. Their plantation owners didn't realize what a powerful learning tool my ancestors possessed. From the Holy Bible, they learned to read and began the process of emancipation for future generations.

Ironically my Great, Great Grandparents would share the same last name; before they were married, they came from Alabama and Maryland. Great, Great Grandmother Rebecca Roberts side of the family began with "Nobody," as well; the census listed people like livestock, so there were no names. It began with a "black female age 5 born in 1855!" Her and several others were listed by age and race on the Federal Census – Slave Schedule of Rebecca Roberts, 1860 United States Division 1, Limestone,

Alabama. The slave owner was listed as R.C. Roberts, and that is where her last name started.

The 1880 United States Census listed Great, Great Grandfather Stan William Roberts, as a barber and a single mulatto male, born in 1854, age 26, Baltimore, Maryland. The son of mulattos' Augustus Roberts, age 58, born in 1822, and Elizabeth Roberts, age 40, born in 1840. Elizabeth was the daughter of a mulatto and my widowed Great, Great, Great Grandmother Rachel Brooks, born 1815 in Baltimore, Maryland. Through slave trade and/or sales during the GSMPM, they would also end up in the Mississippi Delta of Green Hill, Yazoo Precinct. In 1872, he would meet and marry a Roberts, my Great, Great Grandmother Rebecca Roberts.

The oldest of their five children, born in October 1873, would later become my Great Grandmother Lizzie

Big Mama

Josephine Roberts (Big Mama). Lizzie was said to be a mulatto descendent of the Blackfeet Indian tribe and would later "spark" with Ike Smith, or Smich, as his last name was once spelled on a federal census report of 1900. He was from Big Mt. Zion, Mississippi, an affluent community of black land owners two miles north of our village and south of the closest town, Louise, Mississippi. They would have three children: Fannie (1880), Retta (1892),

44

Lem Fountain

and Emely (1896). Retta, the second oldest of three girls, would marry Lem Fountain the second oldest child of Louis and Rebecca Fountain sharecroppers and became my Grandmother Retta Fountain. Not before some serious controversy!

Lizzie Josephine Fountain. The fifth Generation! "Madear," as she was called by all. My mother was born September 6, 1913. Like my direct descendants, she was born on the same plantation and house, "The *Big House, Grandma Retta's House*," by a midwife, Nancy Hughes.

Thomas Woodrow Wilson, a Democrat in Baltimore, won the nomination for president on the 46th ballot and went on to defeat Roosevelt and Taft in that Presidential election. Our country was going through a transition. Unfortunately, those changes, although well intended, did not alter the course of my ancestors' community or sharecropping history for generations to come.

My mother, her sisters and brothers were still seen as nothing but insignificant sharecroppers- a.k.a. "Nobodies"; poor people without an education, destitute, with nothing to offer "Mother America" except their unbreakable labor, a way of life in those horrible steamy hot Delta cotton fields. Every generation of my family was looked down upon by many whites and some affluent blacks, including some of Grandma Retta's family, as those "sharecroppers" or simply "those poor Fountains," the lowest of the lower class working on the half! Many in Grandma Retta's family never forgave her for marrying Grandpapa Lem. And I know that God made all his children equal, so what was so wrong with them being in love with each other?

A generation still enslaved to illiteracy

Befittingly! A heart wrenching and overwhelming story of an arranged marriage within an affluent black socioeconomic group that led to a real shotgun wedding for the "Love" of a poor uneducated sharecropper. Opposites do attract. And it did with repercussions. As the folklore was told, Grandma Retta was secretly forced to marry a black gentleman of affluent status whom she did not love! They were married for three days before Grandpa Lem learned of that marriage.

Captivated by the love they had for each other, Grandpa Lem, at age 21, with shotgun in hand, proceeded to the home of said affluent gentlemen and took Retta, age 18, away from him; allegedly, they had that marriage annulled! Without firing a single shot. Lem and Retta were then married a few weeks later, in the summer of 1911—can you say a real shotgun wedding? I can! From that union, twelve children were born, seven boys and five girls, with my mother, Lizzie Josephine Fountain, born September 6, 1913, being the second oldest and the oldest girl. Grandpa Lem and Grandma Retta worked as sharecroppers on the same land as did his parents for their entire lives. They never wavered from their responsibility of fatherhood and motherhood, even though allegedly Grandpa Lem had strayed from his marriage vows on several occasions.

Some would say that in place of a "well-off" lifestyle, Grandmother Retta chose a humble sharecropper passage filled with manual labor. But I would say it was filled with life's essence, and most important of all, Love. It was jam-packed with many memories, both good and bad, and a large loving family that constantly struggled to make ends meet in a way that most of us simply cannot imagine today. Working from sunup to sundown picking and chopping cotton as their fingers, back, shoulders and neck ached continuously.

Lem's Ledger

My Grandparents were free but still enslaved by forced illiteracy and its ugly byproducts. There was no opportunity to obtain an education under the sharecropping regime that was run by the Jim Crow Law of the Mississippi Delta. My grandparents, as sharecroppers, had now become the same byproduct as Grandpa Lem's ancestors had become, enslaved for labor. The only differences were the scheme of working "on the half" to obtain that promised shared profit: two mules, forty acres of land, and others resources to work the land that one day would be theirs. Guess what: it never HAPPENED! They never received any of the above named promises or any ownership status for their hard labor. Without land of their own, my grandfather and other black families in our community were drawn into sharecropping where they worked a portion of the land owned by "the Boss Man" for a share of the profit from the crops. Anchor Curve was not that fabled land of opportunity, but the birth place of generations of sharecroppers.

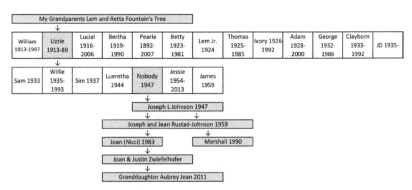

Grandma Retta willingly embraced the role of caregiver for our family as well as her community family.

Grandma would walk miles to help out with what needed to be done to assist the sick or any person in need. She would cook, serve them, and clean up afterwards after working all day in the cotton fields. In addition, she was often called upon to care for her grandkids while Mom worked as the nanny for another plantation owner's kids whenever they went out to parties with their friends to Yazoo City or Jackson Mississippi.

Ever since I can remember, I had always lived with Grandma Retta, and we had such great times together. We would start our days off with a cup of Folgers coffee. She would let me put lots of sugar and some sweet and rich Carnation condensed milk in mine. She would drink hers with just a touch of the condensed milk. Over the next few years, she made sure that I cut back on the amount of sugar and milk I used! After we finished with our daily chores of cooking, cleaning, sewing, and washing, she would some-times send me to the Wilson's store to buy ice cream and bananas. This was a real treat for me. The times we had together were so special for both of us. I believe that those times helped ease some of her burdens: marrying the man she really loved without her family's blessing; dealing with the gossip of her husband's alleged betrayal and infidelity; and seeing no way out of the sharecropping regime of her-self or her children, but the hope was there for her grand-children. She was no doubt an angel of God who brought so much joy to the lives many. Grandma Retta Smith-Fountain went home to be with God on Friday, January 24, 1964. We said our final goodbyes at her funeral on February 8, 1964. What a loss to our family; she was its backbone. Just four years later, Grandpa Lem went home also to be with God in August 1978.

Chapter 3

A JOURNEY OF ESSENCE...

Psalm 27:14 "Wait on the Lord; be of good courage..."

I n God's eyes, we all are created equal: the poor, the rich, the evil, and the good. But man let Satan place a division between the "haves and the have-nots" that created wickedness and righteous ever since the first encounter in the Garden of Eden. This is why our mother always taught us that we must treat each person by

Lizzie Josephine Fountain

the content of a loving heart; the color of an individual's skin does not define their character – even though this was a time when the color of your skin literally determined where you worked, sat, ate, and lived. Luckily, however, Mom dreamed of better things for my sister, five brothers, and me.

In our community, opportunities for black people were few, unless one aspired to spend his or her life working in vast, steamy, and blistering heat, so hot it caused a river of black sweat to flow from your backs in cotton fields full of bloodthirsty mosquitoes, horseflies, and snakes, a few venomous. Not to mention the hot, dusty roads and the furrows or trenches that outlined rows of those awful cotton fields; it was like walking in hot ashes.

As you know by now, Mom was a sharecropper. My father, whom I never knew or had had a relationship with, was said to have been a hardworking man who had a great passion for his freedom to travel and couldn't commit to the life of a sharecropper. His thirst for freedom gave him the opportunity to travel through Mississippi and Texas. People have often said that I cannot miss what I never had, but that is not totally accurate. To be honest, I don't know the truth about my father; some of the stories I have heard were different than what my birth certificate shows, like the story about how my nickname became "Red" for a time. I understood that it was my father who was processing my hair; more to come on this story. To this day, no one will talk about it with me. From my viewpoint I did miss not having a sound male figure of fatherhood in my life; someone who could have been a positive influence and helped with things that a father should have been able to give mature advice on.

In those days, Madear was the go-to person in our community and home. In her role as matriarch, she helped care for the newborn, the sick, the elderly, and anyone else in need. By profession, my mother was a hard worker and expert cotton picker, cook, maid, caterer of food, and caretaker; a father and mother to us. For her labors, she earned burns on her arms from the kitchen stoves; her fingers would crack from the pricks of picking cotton; and nothing could take away the backbreaking pains from the nonstop stooping and bending she endured in those appalling, hot cotton fields all day long without any shaded places to rest. It seemed as if she had been branded with insignias of a sharecropping sorority. She earned a measly three cents per pound for cotton picking and thirty cents per hour for chopping cotton.

Seldom did she see any of the actual money. Instead, she received "Orders" (credit) at the neighborhood grocery store, which was owned by the cotton plantation's family in the Craig Community. At the end of each month, her orders were ostensibly "totaled up," and rarely if ever exceeded the amount she was told that she earned. Mother accepted, having no options, and took whatever amount the "Boss Man," Mr. Macklin, decided to give her.

As an excellent cook and seamstress!

Mom was able to earn a little extra money cooking delightful soul food for the local gentry. She taught us her art of soul food cooking: southern fried chicken, pork chops, and fish; homemade cornbread; banana pudding; chocolate, caramel, and coconut cakes; pumpkin, blackberry, sweet potato pies, and peach cobblers. And to wash it all down with homemade fresh southern lemonade that would be enough to whet anyone's appetite. It seemed that she was always wrist deep in flour from baking, especially when cooking at those social gatherings for the plantation owners or Sunday when the preacher came to supper or at Christmas time.

All told, she made barely enough to support us, though I never knew it. As I look back on our Mom, Grandma Retta and our adventures, and where their lives took them; whether to the forsaken cotton fields; the hot kitchen of their home or the rich plantation kitchens; or to the washtub and washboard, what an adventure! Our daily task was to work in the fields from sunup to sundown, with little time in between to cook, wash, sew, and take care of all the things that required their attention. I witnessed Mom and Grandma walking miles to help sick friends, even those who had wronged or hurt them in some fashion or form; they never held a grudge or talked bad about anyone.

Another thing they did to help our family and community was to piece quilts. Picture the "Big House" living room with its high wood plank ceiling. Hanging from that ceiling was often a quilt in the making. It was strung from four corners of the room. They would sew together scrap pieces of material of different colors and sizes to make two sheets. Then they would take cotton and pick out the seeds and pull it to fluff it to make the padding. There were 4 rails that were seven to eight feet long that were used as stretchers and they would take pieces of twine to attach to the rails and the corners of the quilt. Once it was stretched, it would be raised to sitting height for sewing. Each women would take a corner and work towards the middle. When they were finished for the day they would use the twine to hang it from the ceiling. I would often help with the needle threading and piecing. It was an enjoyable sight to see it hanging over our heads at the end of the day. This is one of my favorite memories about the "Big House."

Since the age of five, I had always been Mom's helper, always working to help her cook, clean, wash, iron, and sew for the plantation owners or the owner of the Anchor Curve's Wilson store. Even though she had to walk miles to and from working at their parties, she could always make a few dollars and occasionally we could bring home some of the leftover food. Being Mom's assistant was an education in itself, which has helped me throughout life. Mom never wanted any of her children, especially her boys, to grow up needing a wife to handle their fundamental necessities. We were all taught to do these essentials for ourselves. My wife will tell you that I handle the essentials most effectively in our family!

Being Madear's helper was not always an easy job. There were always possibilities of negative repercussions if I didn't know "my place." The family that Mom regularly cooked and cared for during their vacations and on weekends had two children, a son my age and a three year old daughter. We had been playmates, but suddenly this all came to screeching halt. During the summer of 1954, at the ripe old age of seven, I began to take on more responsibility as the "water boy" in the cotton fields. I was no longer able to help mom at the parties, and at the time I couldn't understand why!

I was also at an age where I was getting interested in playing sports. But having spent most of my time in the kitchen with Mom and Grandma Retta, I was ill-prepared for playing basketball or baseball, and football was out of the question. So when it came time to pick teams, you can guess where I landed. Let's just say, "Not first" and leave it there. I still sought the reason why I couldn't go with Mom to cook for those parties any more. Was it because I did a bad job on some of my chores and Mom had gotten in some trouble because of it? Or did I occasionally eat too much leftover food?

So began the two different worlds of being "Nobody." And I didn't know which one I belonged to. I didn't know for sure why I could no longer be Mom's helper. Mom just said, "One day you will understand." Meaning that I was getting to the age where I couldn't be trusted to be a playmate with white children, especially a girl. Ironically, I would later marry one, *a white woman!* Another irony was that I used to have nightmares of white people's skin color rubbing off on me!

VIS–A–VIS! I, being raised in single-parent homes, many experts would say that my outcome in life should be one of failure. But being born and raised in a single-parent home helped to prepare me for success and deflated the myths behind single-parenthood homes. Even though academically uneducated, Mom put everything she had into making sure that her children got the opportunity to become whatever they wanted to become in life. As the fifth oldest child of seven growing up in a single-parent household only aided by a grandma, Mom was the primary provider, and this was not with an undemanding effort on her part! She was our strength, hope, role model, and spiritual leader all rolled up into one.

I believe so strongly to this day

Mom knew how slavery and sharecropping had affected many males. This is why she remained a single parent for so many years. She wanted to avoid that kind of husband/fatherless figure for us. She wanted a husband who projected a fatherly image for her children to emulate because she was a God-fearing, strong willed woman who loved her children dearly.

I applaud her for staying a single parent and being that strong motherly image we so desperately needed rather than living in a contentious, dysfunctional home environment just for show! As a single parent, she gave us the love and kindness that many other children in our community wanted. I believe that is why everyone called her "Madear," referring to her as their mother, too; they knew they could count on her. Growing up in a single-parent house, I learned at an early age from Mom and Grandma Retta how important it is to have God and Christ in my life. These were the lessons of two extraordinary women, Mom and Grandma. Their and my brother Willie's words of wisdom still ring true to this day. Willie would say, "Your reputation is your signature for life!" Mom and Grandma kept telling me, "Do not give up on your dreams," "Trust in God and Christ with all your heart and soul; be a good child, a good man and a good father to your children. Teach the children the way of the Lord, as you were taught." "*He might not come when we want Him to, but He is always on time.*" Even though I never knew my biological father, I had the great privilege of being the son and grandson of two great caring and God-fearing women who made sure that we all had opportunities to become successful in life.

The only thing I believe I truly missed by not having a father around was a fatherly image. My brothers, uncles, cousins, coaches, and basketball mentors were my male role models. They helped mold my male image. The only problem with that was they were not always around. Not having a fatherly figure in the home eliminated that sharing experience between a father and the loving and sharing interaction between a mother, a father, a husband, and wife. In order to really appreciate how strikingly and uniquely important the responsibility Mom and other women took on, one needs only to consider that, for centuries, family homes had been decidedly male dominated. So what accounted for the extraordinary achievements by these spirited single-parents? God!

Prized Possession

After emancipation, my ancestors, my grandparents, my mother, and her siblings had to endure that same kind of supervision, eliminating any attempts at education. No matter how "kindly" a slave or plantation owner might have appeared to be, my relatives did not obtain the prized possessions that many sought: freedom and education. The same could be said for my Mom and her siblings, as well as for me, my brothers, and sister. As poor sharecroppers, we were held in bondage through lack of education and never-ending debt, thanks to being basically forced to shop at the "Company Store" (Wilson's).

Old folks, along with my brothers and sister, would also speak of the harsh conditions and the absence of true freedom and how powerless we and our ancestors were under the regimes of slave owners and today's pseudo-slavery establishment: the plantation owners or migrant workers.

Reflecting upon the conditions suffered by my ancestors, I occasionally stare out the window into my garden and contemplate God's beautiful creations. In my personal world, some days are much more beautiful than others. Those special days are filled with gorgeous blue skies and radiating sunshine, punctuated with stunning white, fluffy clouds floating across the horizon like sweet dreams. At other points, there are the ones filled with the dark rainy days with threatening clouds that rumble across the sky like weather nightmares, spouting rain, thunder and lighting, and fierce winds that just say, "seek shelter," or simply stay indoors and sleep. This fear was nothing in comparison to what my ancestors must have felt when the slave traders came rumbling to invade their African communities; being herded into the stench-filled hold of a slave ship where many died of disease or mistreatment during their nine to ten months voyage to America. It must have been a dreadful experience. Then, being marched across a slave auction stage like livestock and being sold to the highest bidder simply added to the horror they must have felt. But through all their trials, tribulations, and the debarking process, they were able to maintain a few traditions: their faith, togetherness, and their delightful style of cooking.

Great Grandma's Gift!

Great Grandma Rebecca's love of African (or soul) food and the way everyone raved about how she could cook is still with me to this day when I think of her, Grandma Retta, and Mom. Grandma Retta and Mom learned from the best and were also outstanding cooks.

Their cooking was sinfully good! As our goods allowed, we would always stuff ourselves. They made the greatest greens, cornbread, southern fried chicken, green tomatoes and okra; sweet potatoes, apple, blackberry, and pecans pies and peach cobblers. Jelly, coconut, chocolate, caramel cakes were also a part of their incredible cooking. Mom also loved cooking and eating collard greens with okra and ham hocks. She would cook the collards and ham hocks for hours, then add some of the lard from the "underside" along with her okra for flavoring.

Our food source came from meats we raised, mostly pork and poultry, and what we caught hunting (rabbits, raccoons) or by fishing. On any given day, alligator gar, bass, bluegill, buffalo, catfish, and/or white perch, might be a part of the day's menu. Home-grown vegetables were also on the menu. We grew cabbage, beets, butterbeans, collard greens, cucumbers, green beans, okra, peas, potatoes, squash, and sweet corn, sweet potatoes, peanuts, tomatoes, and watermelon, rutabaga, and turnip greens – whatever was in season.

Our breads came from corn and wheat that was ground at the local gristmill in exchange for half the yield. It seemed that everything we did or owned was on a so-called "half and half" basis. But we sharecroppers very seldom actually got a real half.

From Great Grandma's recipes, Mom made her homemade biscuits, cornbread, cakes, and pies from scratch. What great cooks they all were! And Mom taught all her children how to cook. A custom passed down over generations.

Just as I had to learn the cooking rituals as passed down from one generation to another, I had to learn the art of "Hog Slaughtering," as well as rabbits, raccoons, and goat skinning. My apprenticeship in these skills began at the ripe old age of ten. On the day of the slaughtering, everyone was up before dawn. A fire would be started around a 20 or 30 gallon wash pot that was filled to the rim with water. Once the water began to boil, it was poured into a very large barrel to place the hog carcass in which was stationed and secured to the ground at a 45 degree angle for easy access. The most skilled and strongest men would then slaughter the hogs using various methods to render them unconscious before landing the fatal blow with a very sharp knife to its gullet. The carcass would then be plunged up and down into the barrel of hot water. This plunging method was used to loosen the hair for ease of removal, leaving the skin smooth and clean. The carcass was then brought to a scaffold for processing. However, the goats would be processed and cleaned using a different method of skinning to remove hair.

No parts of the carcasses were wasted. We used the fat from the underbelly of the hogs to make lard and shortening for cooking cakes and other delicious foods. The lard was stored in various tin buckets that resembled paint cans. The skin made especially good cracklings after being cooked in a large pot and separated from the grease. After the cracklings had cooled, the women ground them up and put them in containers and stored in a cool place. Later, it would be used for seasoning vegetables and making crackling cornbread. Other parts of the hogs were used for such things as: sausage, hog's head souse, or cheese and hams.

The hams and shoulders sides were used for bacon and fatback. They were all rubbed with salt and prepared for hanging in the smoke house. The meat was left to hang in the smoke house until it was used. Some hams were carefully wrapped in clean cloth and left to cure. The goat meat was cured using some of the same processes, such as salting and smoking, or simple air-drying processes. Rabbits, raccoons, and goats had to be skinned and usually cooked immediately or no later than a few days.

Are we there YET...Nobody!

Chapter 4

THE SIXTH GENERATION – MY BEGINNING‼

My life [Joseph Lewis Johnson] began at 4 a.m. on November 10, 1947. My birthplace was the large bedroom in the Big House, located deep in the cotton fields of Anchor Curve, Mississippi. Anchor Curve was and still is a tiny, unincorporated village some four miles southeast of the town of Louise, Mississippi. The Big House then was my grandparent's home, where three previous generations were born. And amazingly, that house stood until 1965, though it was in much need of a makeover in its last days.

Anchor Curve itself was a tiny, unincorporated community consisting of a small cluster of houses (including the Big House) and surrounded by an endless sea of cotton fields in the steamy Mississippi flatlands known as The Delta.

The Mississippi Delta lies between the Mississippi and Yazoo rivers. Thanks to cheap labor, rich soil, and proximity to the huge tow-boats and barges that ply the Mississippi and Yazoo rivers, the Delta was, and still is, the heart of America's cotton belt. Sadly, it remains one of the poorest regions in the United States.

Al's House

This is a photo of my best friend Alford ("Al") Smith's home, taken in 1972. It looks exactly the same as the Big House. It was just that: BIG! (At least it seemed huge back then, especially to a scrawny little kid.)When I wasn't with Grandma Retta or Mom helping out around the Big House, I spent a great deal of my time at my friend Al's house, which was the place to be, especially during the harvest seasons. In the back of his house, there were apple and peach tree orchards. It was from Al's house that we watched our older brothers and their friends go swimming in Silver Creek and play cat and mouse games with the girls in the neighborhood who congregated at the house across the street from Al's, the Mays' house.

Like many old southern homes, the large kitchen was separated from the house and the main gathering place for our family. The tin roof rattled in the wind, leaked in the rain, and roared like a train when it rained or hailed. All twelve of us at one time or another (immediate and extended family) were packed into that four-room wooden house without the benefit of a single indoor bathroom or plumbing. Instead, we had an outhouse that was located at the end of a well-worn path several yards behind the Big House's kitchen and was not the most pleasant place to be.

Our plumbing consisted of an outdoor water pump that kicked like a mule when it needed priming (*this consisted of pouring water into it while pumping the handle extremely fast to remove any air pressure left inside, in order to retrieve water from it*). On more times than I care to remember, that pump fought back during "*priming,*" with powerful blows to my chin as my powerless hands could not handle its kickbacks in my attempts to prime it. Nonetheless, it was a cherished home to several generations of my family, including my Grandparents, Mom, Aunts, Uncles; three older brothers

Sam, Willie and Sim; my only sister, Lueretha; and two younger brothers, Jessie and James.

I am the fifth of seven children, six boys and one girl, born into an impoverished sharecropper's family. While continuing to fight the prejudice of poverty and social injustice, Mom decided to name me after two great men, one being my Great Grandfather Robert "Lewis" Fountain, a man of great character and faith. Also during this time in history there was another man of great character that fought social injustice in a different way and offered hope to so many, "Joe" Louis Barrow, better known as "The Brown Bomber," one of the greatest prize fighters of all time. So from these two great men's names came my name, Joseph Lewis Johnson.

I did have several nicknames; friends called me Red because I had red hair from a bad hair straightening process and the sun bleaching it. They actually had to put my head in a tub of cold water to stop it from stinging! My mom was really upset. For a time, I was also called Goat Jones by friends and family; more to come on this story. More prominently, friends and family called me Skeeter; some still do to this day. I like to think it is because of my great basketball skills, being able to smoothly skeet the ball into the net, but my family might tell you this nickname came from a more base bodily function that I apparently did well!

An early Tall Tail

As the story goes, Mom and Grandma Retta had used one of the old family recipes for oven roasted goat meat they had gotten from a neighbor named Mr. Jones. Even before the cooking process began, the aroma of their wonderful recipe began to fill the kitchen. Everyone hurried to complete their chores in anticipation of this wonderful meal. As they began to roast the goat meat, its aroma filled not only the kitchen, but the whole house and outside as I played. Smelling that delicious aroma made it seem like it took forever to cook, but it only took a few hours. Finally, when that mouth-watering meal was ready to eat, everyone except for Uncle Clay was there for supper. He had gone to see his wife-to-be, Earl Anne Rose. So as a lover of Mom and Grandma's cooking, especially this day having roasted goat meat, and in order for me to get more of it, I had to wait until Uncle Clay came home for his supper, usually just before bed time. I knew that he would share his supper with me as a rule since I was his favorable nephew, or so he said! He would often take me with him when he went sparking with his wife-to-be. Those five mile walks to her house down that lonely gravel road at early dusk seemed short and pleasant with Uncle Clay. But the return walks were in pitch black darkness without any light except for the light of God's moon lighting our path. The gravel road also made it very difficult to walk on at night, not to mention cotton fields lined each side of us with an occasional house without lights, too.

Therefore, our ten o'clock pm return trip home for me seemed like an eternity filled with frightening anxiety with every step. It was almost as frightening as hearing those ghost tales about the casting of evil romantic spells. That night, by the time Uncle Clay got home I was very tired. Before we could finish eating his supper, I fell asleep with a goat bone in my mouth and slept with it there throughout the night. When I woke up the next morning, I was given the nickname of Goat Jones. Since that time, and even throughout high school, to those who knew me well (mostly family members) occasionally they still called me Goat Jones to humor themselves. This was just another embarrassing moment in time in my life, with several more to come.

Gift of Grandpa Lem's Philosophy...

Every family has its philosophers; my Grandfather Lem was ours. I still embrace his worldly Wisdom in my heart and it helped me to define my and my family's life. He would always say "Blessed Boy"...!

"Don't fatten frogs up for snakes."

Don't take your hard-earned money and use it on something that will not benefit you.

"An empty wagon makes a lot of noise."

The empty wagon philosophy means... Let your character speak for you. Men that don't have great wisdom of character are like an empty wagon rolling down a rough road, making a great deal of noise and not accomplishing anything of importance!

"A dog is going to need his tail more than once to shoo the nits from around his...!"

If a dog uses his tail only one time to shoo away life's infestations, he loses the important reasons why God gave it to him. So don't just pray one time for something but pray repeatedly until what you are praying for is received.

"If you play with a dog, he will lick your mouth; and if you play with a child, he will sass you out."

Playing with a dog even with or without discipline, he will surely lick your mouth, but if you play with child without discipline, he surely will sass you out. Sparing the rod of chastening surely will spoil a child.

"Don't get bit by the same dog, in the same place and time."

Why do we continue down that same old road? If you routinely get bitten by the same dog, how can you progress in life? We can't do it alone; we need God, who strengthens us to be less of a sinner and more than conquer.

"Don't air your dirty laundry in the community."

Take it to God; He won't judge and will make it spotless, people judge!

As Sharecroppers…

As slave laborers, my foreparents were indoctrinated with the idea that either they couldn't learn or that they simply didn't need to learn how to read and write. They were classified as uneducated laborers suitable only for field work or housework. Illiteracy was an accepted way of life as well as a controlling mechanism for slave owners.

It began for my Great, Great grandparents as slavery ended. But frankly, as I stated earlier, there wasn't much difference between the two at the time. What I do know was that generations of American sharecroppers, including my mother and her siblings, were paid so little they could barely survive.

Yes! I am the sixth generation descendant of slaves. I know this with certainty from the documentation of my ancestors' history authenticated by the United State Federal Census (1860 –1900) including Slave Schedule Registers. I confirmed that my ancestors' historical travel encompassed a passage that took them from Africa to America followed by the SGMPM that took place around 1790 and lasted almost a century and took them from the states of Alabama, North and South Carolina, Maryland, and Virginia, enslaving them in the 1850s in the rural communities of Woolfolk and Gibbs of Yazoo County, Mississippi. Following the failure of both the contract labor system and land reform after the Civil War (1861-65), they turned to sharecropping as inhabitants of Yazoo County that encompassed Green Hill, Craig Community, and Anchor Curve, Mississippi.

My ancestors' faith in God and Christ helped them to persevere through the Deep South's insidious but subtle curse of slavery. After the Civil War, a new form of slavery evolved and is still with us today in this country and others. I call it Slavery Lite! Most people call it sharecropping or migrant work! There probably were, and still are, some fair and legitimate sharecropping and migrant work situations today in America. However, this menacing scheme kept my family members and many others enslaved to a way of life that left a trail of deprived uneducated people for five long and miserable generations.

Fortunately for us, Mom wanted more, and so did my siblings and I. We also inherited our ancestors' faith in God and Christ as well as their will to persevere, which equipped me to become a college graduate with a Masters, a teacher's aide, and an educational entrepreneur to 175 nontraditional children and their families.

It is hard for me to believe and understand that there are still so many minority adolescents and their families having to come face to face with this same deceptive but yet subtle enemy that I was forced to face and endure growing up as a sharecropper's son in the late 40s, 50s, and into the 60s. It is also hard to believe that these enemies of mine that seriously damaged and held a vice on my formative school years can still flourish in a contemporary America.

The grueling tasks of plantation work is always accompanied by illiteracy due to denied educational opportunities by the means of seriously abbreviated school years. This was one of the main adversities that hindered my life, as it did many others. Illiteracy stalked and attempted to capture me in its claws of hopelessness, as it did many of my ancestors.

Have we, as contemporary America, allowed child labor to continue? I believe so strongly that each adolescent, no matter where their geographic birth took place or the circumstances surrounding it, has the potential to be a productive citizen in our society with the proper education, regardless of who their parents are. In him or her lies the possibility of greatness to be carved out. But like the sins of slavery that birthed greed and pride, leaving all this potential without education, and without it we are now losing some of the world's great minds, our children. Yet we are amazed at how other countries have passed us academically when we are losing such great minds to what...! And why?

During our life at Anchor Curve, we were not only worked to exhaustion, fed on a starchy diet, paid meager wages, and doused with pesticides like DDT, but also much later in life, I, like many of my uncles, was driven to early alcohol and drug abuse, leading to degenerating sickness like diabetes. Also a significant number of my classmates' relatives were driven to an early death for the same reasons.

We had to endure labor harshness, which was often carried out in weather conditions that were unbearable due to the extreme heat. For example, a regular work day often consisted of 10 to 12 hours a day in temperatures that often exceeded 100 degrees under a blue sky and a blistering sun. Our work habits often involved constant bending, carrying heavy items, and repetitive motions throughout long working hours, which contributed to injuries of both the back muscles and vertebrae. So where was that relief from such hard labor; believe it or not, those that didn't know God found only temporary relief that perpetuated itself on the street of our hometown, Louise, or the surrounding run down juke joints (bars).

During my Anchor Curve preteen years, something became very evident to me. The major difference between a growing child's successes or failures was having loving, positive, strong people to listen, guide, and support them. Children can't do it alone – nor should they have to! While I personally experienced the pains of poverty and the evil of prejudice, I was also fortunate enough to experience the unconditional love and kindness of my family and many others who unselfishly helped me grow and succeed as a child. They made me strong. They showed me what it meant to be respected and to give respect. They made it clear how important education was to getting ahead in life. They helped me navigate the trials and tribulations of my youth to become an empowered pre-adult.

Chapter 5

MY HOMETOWN

By 1918, the communities in our county were rezoned and renamed Humphreys County after B. G. Humphreys, a colonel for the Confederate Army and governor of Mississippi from 1865-68. Louise's population was approximately 700 people. The plantations and the affluent black farm communities had a population of approximately 150 people living in some of the top graded bottom land suited for raising cotton. Anchor Curve's Craig Community, Green Hill, Woolfolk, and Gibbs made up part of what was once Yazoo County.

Louise Business District

Main Street consisted of a post office, two furniture stores, two grocery stores owned by Chinese families, and a drug store that doubled as the Greyhound Bus station. Louise's ice cream parlor and café boasted the conventional "whites only" and "blacks only" signs displayed in the proper sections, as well as the only café and the only movie theater. The only employment was the dusty, noisy cotton gins; one located along the railroad tracks on the south edge of the towns' business district, and another on the northwest end of town.

West of the railroad tracks was the entertainment district, consisting of two dubious run-down juke joints where one could drink, gamble, fight, and be entertained by ladies of questionable morals. Louise was a totally segregated town.

Its residential districts consisted of neighborhoods all segregated and separated by Main Street. On the southwest end of town across Silver Creek, you had the more affluent black residents: the teachers, the land owners, the small neighborhood merchants, and a barbershop, a small grocery store owned and operated by a blind man, the preachers, and the plantation owners' full-time housekeepers.

At the opposite end of town, the northeast was another black neighborhood that consisted of middle to lower class residents, a few teachers, and mostly day workers who hired out their services to other farmers and plantation owners and worked at the cotton gins.

And of course, everything east of Main Street belonged to the whites, the Chinese families, the plantation owners, the proprietors, the white teachers, the merchants, and the town civic leaders. They all lived in lovely brick and colonial-style homes with well-kept cosmetic lawns and gardens, cultivated weekly by their black gardeners and lawn boys like me. Their children attended Humphrey County Elementary, Middle and High School that took on the same facade as their cosmetic lawns, gardens, and brick homes. The high school even had a football stadium and lights, a state-of-the-art track-and-field facility that bordered the southeast end of town in clear view of our makeshift grounds where we played football, baseball, and ran track. And if that wasn't bad enough, we received their hand-me-down books and sports equipment.

There were farming communities less than a mile north of town across the railroad tracks. This was where Mr. Hudy Montgomery resided. He was a very wealthy but an extremely generous black man. Mr. Montgomery donated large sums of money to build our school and gymnasium, which was named after him. Also within that community were other sharecropping communities that would later become part of my life and home to us. In addition, one of those was the site for the Freedom Rider rally, which came to Louise in the mid-1960s after two local black men were murdered.

On those hot and steamy Saturday evenings after working all week, many sought Louise as the place to be to let off a little steam and have some fun. As I look back on those days, a Saturday night in Louise was filled with adventure and fear. There were people from within an easy walking distance, to some as far as ten miles away. This "One Horse Town Main Street" was a happening place for people from those black communities, as well as a dangerous place. The only whites or Chinese that were seen on Main Street were its merchants or an occasional white teen or young adult who stopped at the ice cream parlor for a treat while attempting to lure one of our beautiful bi-racial sisters into taking a ride with him. But the majority of white teens and young adults went to Belzoni, Yazoo City, or Jackson for their weekend fun, leaving Louise's Main Street to us.

A Thriving Small Town

If other teenagers and I were fortunate enough to have earned some extra money after working all day Saturday at another plantation, we had an opportunity to indulge in some of Louise's delicious treats: foot-long hot dogs; chocolate-dipped ice cream cones; pineapple, butterscotch and strawberry milkshakes; and fruit flavored sodas with peanuts poured into the bottle. What a carefree moment in time this was for us as we would stroll up and down crowded Main Street from the ice cream parlor to the post office on the north end of town. Great times! Great fun! I was able to put away unpleasantness for that short-lived moment in time. Probably just like the older men of Louise who sought to ease their pains in the juke joints. But what Mom and the other mothers did to ease their pain was God and Christ! I never saw or heard of Mom using alcohol to ease her pains, and she had plenty.

Also, during my strolls up and down Main Street, I employed my Perry Mason detective skills to study the older boys and how they maneuvered after their prey, the girls. They waited for that special opportune moment to attract the attention or catch the eye of that special girl without their parents being aware. I thought what a thrill it must have been playing those cat-and-mouse games. However, on occasion some ended up with an occasional baby being born out of wedlock. This caused great problems in the athletic ranks between friends on the football and basketball teams, especially if their sister was the mouse caught by that sly cat.

All of those black souls, young and old, who would walk up and down the main street of Louise, gave the distinct impression that they were looking for something that they could never find–freedom? Or possibly it could have been just peace of mind from the stress of life as a smallholder. Those horrifying work conditions from early morning chilly dew, to the midday heat index of triple digits, to the exhaustion of a ten to twelve hour back-breaking work day left many with the distinct impression of being less than a man or a woman and not being able to see their way out of their current and desperate situations. Like any stressful situation, this kind did not discriminate. It attacked and captivated across all races and social lines. It engulfed and devastated the already deprived poor, who were trying so desperately to find the shores of prosperity from a sea of poverty. The affluent tried desperately not to become overwhelmed themselves, like the poor had been, by closely scrutinizing who their children formed relationships with or befriended.

Then you had the proprietors, the town civic leaders, and Main Street merchants with their pompous wheeling and dealing. Constantly trying to feed their greed by means of our parents' hard labor; who were only trying to make the best living possible for themselves and their families. It was as if their greed and pride were sucking the life out of Main Street, and they weren't giving anything back to the survivability of Louise's Main Street.

Women of Louise

In those days, parents did not accept the casual ways that boys and girls befriend each other, let alone get involved in serious relationships. They were much, much more protective of their daughters and demanded to know who the boy was that approached her and for what reason. Our parents did not give that consent without first knowing the male and his parents. Of course, we all learned to maneuver around parents' strict rules! I had learned my strategy from some of the best, and being an outstanding jock paid great dividends, especially after games and prom night. From our parents' perspective, it was a time of great concern, to say the least, for our safety and wellbeing as well as policing their daughters' acquaintances.

Shopping for the best deal they could find, with limited money they had earned for that weeks' work, was another unavoidable task. You see, the stores in Louise were not tailored for purchasing school supplies and clothing for sharecroppers like us. They catered to the elite. There were no department stores in the town of Louise, just the two Chinese grocery stores that sold a few clothes of farming quality. For that reason, the few clothes that we bought had to be purchased in Yazoo City, which had department stores that were more suitable for shopping for school, church, and other non-farming functions, and had better and more affordable selections of apparel to choose or pick from.

Sharecroppers like Mom could only clothes-shop once a year in Yazoo City, after the entire crop was harvested in January. In case of an emergency, Mom could sometimes beseech the Big Boss Man for a few dollars. Unfortunately for us, that time always came at the end of the year, and then he wouldn't settle up with her until after the New Year. Ninety percent of the time, she owed him money from the pleading, so what were we working for? The answer was mainly shelter because we grew most of our food and our clothing was hand-me-down or what Mom made! Christmas around our house for the most part was celebrated without any new things, no toys and clothing. This didn't mean that we had a bad Christmas, because we did not; just some disappointments of not having toys and stuff like the other children. However, those disappointments later on were a blessing in disguise because they helped me to define my life and prepared me for life's misfortunes of not having things you wanted, and to be thankful for what you had.

My Mother's Ledger

Mom made sure that the true spirit of Christmas was enjoyed by having a feast to celebrate and honor Jesus' birthday. She would cook for what seemed like days, preparing a meal of her home made jelly, coconut, chocolate, and caramel cakes; collard greens with ham hocks and okra; southern fried chicken; chicken and cornbread stuffing; sweet potatoes, apple, blackberry, and pecans pies and peach cobblers. Her cooking would fill our house with an aroma that was fit for God and Christ. We would always stuff ourselves. And it would be enough to last through the New Year week. We didn't have much to celebrate with but we truly had God's blessing to have her for our mother. She was our mother, father, and provider who cared for us when sick and protected us from the evil of this world by faith and belief in Christ. But we also had some fun when she would debunk the ghostly tall tales of Anchor Curve.

Some Tall Tales of Anchor Curve

I was born in an era when one's entertainment was not from various HD television shows, PlayStations, Game Boys, or Xboxes–just ghostly sagas. Tall tales were one of the main methods of entertainment. The groundwork for telling those tall tales was that there were two cemeteries that bordered the cotton fields where we worked and lived. Those spine tingling and back-of-the-neck hair-raising tales were told best by our community's elders, especially Mrs. Cindy Woods. Mrs. Woods would also tell tales of women that would put "voodoo" on men. They would use chicken feet and sprinkle special love potions in your food to control you. She would say that this voodoo would make you run wild through the woods and eat Bessie bugs that live in or between wet logs and various worms, etc. On our front porch, The Big House, everyone sat around a large washtub that had old quilts, shoes, and just rags in it that had been doused with a little coal oil to get the fire going. Before the fire would grow in intensity, it was smothered causing smoke to fill the area acting as an insecticide, to get rid of mosquitoes, as she told of how the dead would return to hunt those who had done them wrong. One of her particularly spine-tingling ghost stories was of this enormous white ghost who was so tall that he could sit on the top of the Big House and his feet would rest on the ground. It terrorized me for years. Of course, there was the story about a particular grave in Yazoo City that had logging chains around it that still concerns me to this day. When I looked it up on the internet, my computer crashed so needless to say, that's all I have to say about that story!!!

Those ghost tales were more frightening than my 10:00 pm walk home down that lonely gravel road with Uncle Clay. Many nights I was unable to sleep unless someone was in the room with me, and my head had to be underneath the bed covering. I would never be caught away from home after dark except for those evenings when, after attempting to do my homework, I would go to Aunt Pearl and Uncle Joe Willie's to watch television. They had the only television in the community. It was a secondhand black-and-white box-shaped TV with a rabbit ear antenna, VHS and UHF 3 channels. I also knew that I had to walk home alone a quarter of a mile when my favorite evening shows, Roy Rogers or Perry Mason, were over. This was only if my brother

Sim and his friends weren't watching their programs: The Twilight Zone, Playhouse 90 or Alfred Hitchcock Presents. After the worst of them, I would risk wetting the bed to avoid going outside at night to the outhouse. I was in fear of those ghostly figures Mrs. Woods described, especially the one so tall that it could sit on top of the Big House and his feet would touch the ground as he waited to take bad children away and their parents would never see them again!

Then there were ghosts of lesser intensity in size, but just as frightening, with the purpose of getting you home before dark. Those lesser intensive tall tales focused on ghosts and spirits that would wait in the cotton fields or along the highway at night with the main purpose of chasing you to see how fast you could run home. My brother knew all along that their favorite TV programs were frightening for me to watch and that I had to walk home alone or stay and receive a punishment from Mom if she had to come to get me after working all those long hours or send my sister, the enforcer! This was just another way that my brother and his friends had fun at my expense. So either choice I made was distressing. If I stayed, I risked punishment from Mom and displeasure from my sister, who had to leave what she was doing to come and get me. Or I walked home alone and was scared to death of those ghosts waiting to get me. Many nights when I thought that I was brave enough to walk home by myself, I ended up setting an all-time record in the quarter-mile run! Especially when unknown things or the wind would cause some of those cotton stalks to all of a sudden jiggle or move like someone was walking along beside me. Then the race home was on as the hair on my neck would stand up and say, let's Go...!!! And the goose bumps that engulfed my entire body said, let's see how fast we can Go...!!! But it was as if I was running for my life in one of those Twilight Zone nightmarish dreams, with feet and legs that seemed like they weighed a ton as I made my mad dash for home, looking back, fearful to see if my ghostly pursuer(s) were gaining on me. Once home, I tried to calm myself to hide my unnerving fears from Mom so I could face the same thing another night after watching my favorite TV shows. It wasn't until I was a freshman in high school before I had conquered my fears of those tall tales!

I learned later that my brother and his friends had experienced similar frightening situations. It was during the time of road construction, and there were tall piles of gravel that lined one side of the road. And one moonlit night as they were walking past those piles, they saw their own shadows being cast by the moon and thought that their shadows were ghosts following them. Therefore, each time they stopped, ran or walked so did their shadows, their ghostly figures! Now scared senseless, they ran home and told Mom how those ghosts were following them. She politely took them back to their ghostly sighting and showed them that it was only their shadows reflecting off the piles of gravel. WOW!

The Men of Louise

With the end of the Korean War, soldiers like my uncles—George Fountain, who was an orderly in an Army Mash Unit; Adam Fountain, who was wounded in a battle with his Amy unit and ended up at Uncle George's Mash

Unit; and Ivory Fountain, who serviced fourteen years in the Marine Core as a sergeant and MP. They eagerly headed back home to start families and fought to carve out their futures as a part of the beginning of the baby boom era. Louise, however, was not the most opportune place in America, unless you had aspirations of becoming a sharecropper or common laborer!

What can I say? As I look back now, I can see why some of the men were attracted to the "entertainment" districts across the railroad tracks and the Roadhouse about two miles south of town. These two run-down juke joints were where they indulged in the temporal spirits of wine, beers, whiskey and other hard liquor such as "moonshine." It wasn't uncommon for them to gamble and fight. As for the Roadhouse outside of the city limits, it attracted the same kind of clientele but focused more on the gambling. These places were also segregated. With the exception of a few whites who might have viewed themselves as compassionate companions or befriended them for an opportunity to be lovers of the black women who were also present. This was an anything-goes type of environment. They knew that as long as they did not kill anyone of important stature, insult a white man, or God forbid, have contact with a white woman that they would not be sought after. Whatever else they did would be overlooked by their Big Boss Men; and they would be able to go home, nap Sunday night and return to work on Monday morning. I believed they thought that their weekend rituals would ease their pains and block out the harsh reality of that week's work and the ones to come.

Now I know why some of my uncles and the other men of Louise used those weekend rituals to defile themselves on a continuous basis. I found myself later on in life participating in the same weekend rituals in the streets of Oakland, Chicago and Madison. Farther along in life, I learned from Pastor Butler, a friend and minister of the church we attended in Wausau, that no sin, no matter how momentarily pleasurable and comforting or how routinely I indulged in them, it wasn't worth missing out on God's blessing.

Normal field hands, a teenager like me, were expected to be able to pick 150 to 200 pounds of cotton per day. Men like my uncle JD would pick as much as 500 pounds daily. It was backbreaking work. From our first sight of the sun in the morning until it was dark, we all harvested cotton, moreover, in the heat of late summer, commonly under a blazing sun whose index some days exceeded 115 degrees by midday. We had to work fast to make our quota and had to work carefully not to incorporate dirt, leaves or trash into our cotton sacks. Teenagers my age were often valued as good cotton pickers because of our ability to stoop lower, and suffered less back pain. Not being able to see any way out of those devastating and desperate situations made it just that much more difficult to get up each morning.

We all, the young and old, males and females, were casualties of the slave and sharecropper eras of low-to-no wages. And to top that off, all black males, regardless of ages were called "boy," which was obviously an insult, adding onto the demoralizing work we did in the cotton fields. Any hope of ever escaping that awful plague would depend totally on educational opportunities, which my descendants did not have. This continual feeling of abandonment and humiliation that they experienced was now trying to place me in its grips as a contemporary laborer.

A Thriving Small Town ends...

By the end of the late 1960s, Main Street stores began to close, just like the movie theater and two cotton gins closed down years earlier, and then the only doctor in town was on his way out. Louise's thriving small business district had started to fade into nothing in front of my eyes. The final nail into the town's Main Street coffin was the emergence of the farm-raised catfish, which took the place of raising cotton for many plantation owners. This new type of farming eliminated countless jobs. By 1976, Louise and Belzoni were the farm-raised catfish capitals of the United States.

Chapter 6

1950S ADVENTURES

Wile E. Coyote Cowboy

December 1952, at the age of five, I was playing a cowboy who was being chased by Indians through the hills (our kitchen) into some big rocks (our living room) of our house. One of the big rocks (a rocking chair) near the fireplace and from behind it I took cover to fight off my hostile pursuers. Therefore, in running to take cover behind the big rock I tripped and went soaring over it face-first toward the fireplace without any hope of not planting my face into it. Fortunately, or maybe it was God's blessing, I stretched out my hands to break my fall, causing them to slide underneath the hot ashes and coals of the burnt wood of the fireplace. I severely burned both of my hands instead of planting my face into those hot ashes and coals! The shock and the pain were over-whelming after I was pulled away from the fireplace, and Mom treated my burned hands with castor oil to reduce the swelling in hope that the skin would recondition itself.

I was also given BC Powder for pain. While searching the internet to make sure I had the name right, to my surprise, I can still get the same BC Powder today for pain and headache relief.

Appropriately, at the age of five I did not know to thank God for His blessing that no major bones were damaged. I would heal quickly without any major visible scars, but I am 100 percent sure that Mom must have thanked Him. I just knew that I was in a great deal of pain and would stay away from fireplaces when playing. It wasn't funny to me or anyone that was present at the time. But I can image later how humorous it must have been seeing me flying through the air head-first over my imaginary big rock toward a fireplace of sizzling hot ashes and coals with no way of stopping, like Wile E. Coyote! This is the first time I recall God saving me for His work.

Mom's Note – Pall Mall!

As I continued in my role as helper, I would take the "Note" (grocery list) to the small neighborhood family grocery store, which was approximately one fourth of a mile away from the Big House. Those chores did not call for one to be able to read and write. Mom, Grandma Retta and others cooked like it was an art, from memory and not written recipes. We could go and purchase groceries or cigarettes from the Wilson's store as long as Mom, using her third-grade education, wrote them the "Note" and signed it, which usually consisted of the same things not grown in our garden and occasionally either ham, sausages, salami, bologna, headcheese and bread for sandwiches; salt, black pepper, sugar and coffee, condensed carnation milk; and Mom's Pall Mall cigarettes. Many days, as I took Mom's Note to the store and watched the storekeeper fill the order, I wished I could have a piece of some hard candy, but it wasn't on the Note. I was scared to death to ask for a piece or try to add it. Each time, after Mrs. Wilson had finished filling the order and giving it to me, she would always say, "Tell Sis (Mom) I say hello and what a nice boy that she has to do her shopping for her." I then would think to myself, "If I'm so damn nice then give me a piece of that hard candy!" It seemed like a thousand times that I took that Note to the Wilson's store. Each time, I would try to think of ways to get some of that hard candy, but I never came up with a concrete solution.

Just like Mom, I never came up with a solid solution to limit walking almost everywhere we went. We had to walk nearly a mile to work the plantation owner's parties, to cook, serve them and then clean up in order to earn a very few extra dollars. A reward for all her hard work was that we could sometimes bring home some leftovers, and that was an okay treat in itself, or receive hand-me-down clothing. She and I would clean up before, during and after the main meal had been served and walk back home. Occasionally, once we had gotten home from those parties, Mom would be so tired that she would just lie on the bed and go to sleep with her work clothes on. This kind of overtaxing lifestyle irritated me greatly that Mom had to work this hard and long to make sure that we had enough to eat, a place to sleep and mostly hand-me-down and cheap clothes to wear. Deep down inside, I knew that Mom was hurting because she'd done the best she could and wasn't able to give us the things that the other children in the neighborhood had. In reminiscing upon these old times, I used to think of my favorite song by Clarence Carter, "Patches," when his dying father called him to his bedside and told him these words: "Patches, I'm depending on You, son, to see the family through. It seemed to be written for me, too. However, we were not as bad off as the lyrics of that song portrayed Patches.

The Stoner family Mom worked for had two children around my age, and Mrs. Stoner would sometimes give Mom food and her son's old clothing to help out. Darning and patching were sometime needed, especially around the knees. So in some form or fashion I was like Patches, who wore ragged but clean clothing. Being her helper was an education in itself for all of her children. It was her way of preparing us to face life's essential challenges. She never wanted any of her children to grow up needing a wife or husband to take care of any of our essential needs, when it came to the fundamentals of cooking, cleaning, darning, washing or ironing.

Big Yellow

The summer of 1954 was one filled with excitement as I prepared for my first day of school. The big day would be September 4th. I could hardly wait! First grade was a happy time, yet sad, too, for my plantation chores were coming to an end until fall harvest time. This would also end my time as Mom's helper at the lavish plantation parties. Now I would get to ride on "Big Yellow," the school bus with my older sister and brothers and all the other children who caught "Big Yellow" at our house.

Our house was what people today would call a duplex or a two family home. There were two main entrances. In between them was an entrance to a small room, Mom's bedroom, separating our side of the duplex from the other side that was occupied by an older lady who Mom cared for! The unique thing about this house was that it was built by Great Grandfather Robert "Lewis" Fountain, and he and Great Grandmother Josephine lived and died there. It had a long front porch. There was no separation of the porch between the front doors. So there was a lot of space for me to run and play. Our side of the duplex had two large windows on each side of our main entrance. From my perspective, our living room was very large with a fireplace. It doubled as one of the two bedrooms and connected to the kitchen. The kitchen was an average size with a table and chairs, and a wood burning stove with four burners, also called "four eyes." Attached to the kitchen was another small room that Mom used as a pantry. Once we finally got electricity, Mom keep a small deep freezer there that she got from Mrs. Stoner. The back of the house was the same as the front. Later, I would build myself a basketball court on our side.

The house was covered with tin without any insulation. And when it rained it sounded like rocks falling from the skies pounding on top of it. Our winters were somewhat cold with light frosted mornings and very occasionally a light snow that only lasted until mid-day. It still took lots of wood burning in the fireplace to heat that old house with no insulation to keep the heat from escaping through its tin top roofing. In the summer, it would be just the opposite. It would be so hot, you could literally cook an egg on the tin top, which I contemplated trying on several occasions but never followed through. I knew that Mom would have hung me if she found me trying to fry an egg on the roof of our house. It was not for the danger but for the ignorance of using one of her good eggs for some kind of experiment.

I had worked hard and waited all summer long for this big day – the first day of school. During that first year, I experienced several things that would change my attitude toward school. Making friends was not going to be easy. I wanted to play sports after seeing my brother Willie make "The Catch" on the baseball diamond, and my brother Sim, "Mr. Cool," on the basketball court. My older brother Sam had moved to Greenville, Mississippi, so I didn't get a chance to see him that much, but I always wanted to go and visit him and Great Grandma, "Big Mama."

My first year experience in school was not a good one and would be that way for decades to come. I was now experiencing some of the disappointing things that my older siblings had already experienced in school. I didn't possess Standard English at an early age that was being spoken in the home of the educated children. For that reason alone, reading and writing then came very hard to me. Most children, the so-called cool ones and the ones from homes which had been exposed to this language at an early age, didn't want to be with someone like me, who spoke in broken sentences and had been labeled as dumb and stupid, "Nobody."

In our community and surrounding communities most families had some formal academic education with the exception of three or four, one being ours. Some had finished high school, attended college and were teachers.

After learning the fundamentals of life from Mom and beginning my academic career, the next challenges were to learn the fundamentals of athletics and sportsmanship. Without a father to teach me these basic skills of playing sports, I turned to my brothers Willie and Sim; my Uncle JD and their friend Boy Blue. To me, they were great! Willie and Uncle JD were two of the greatest baseball players, while Sim and Boy Blue were the greatest on the basketball court.

Second Grade

I did not know which one of my second grade initiations terrified me the most, having to look out for snakes during my "water boy" treks, or those dreadful days at school filled with embarrassment, namely Wednesday's "Corporal Punishment" (a.k.a. the dreaded spelling quiz) days, as I dubbed them. This day was the most frightening and embarrassing time for myself and others like me, who had a difficult time comprehending standard teaching methods of using memorization skills, especially when it came to spelling quizzes. I did not know that I was suffering from learning disabilities, inattentive distraction, a form of Attention Deficit Disorder coupled with dyslexia, which required a systematic approach to learning, especially spelling. Therefore, I had to endure this ritual until freshmen year in high school.

Our educational system didn't know the adage, "If a child isn't learning, check the teaching." With certain teachers in our school, if a poor child had problems learning, it was the student's or the parent's fault, and if that child regularly scored below 70%, as I did, on their Wednesday spelling quizzes, they would get a spanking, lashing or a beating that day from the hand of that teacher. This thrashing would consist of as many lashes as she, the teacher, deemed necessary using a cotton gin strap, three-sixteenth of an inch thick and a width of four inches. Those harsh punishment and abuse occurred in front of my classmates and any other students or teachers who might just happen to be passing by our classroom at that specific time. What they would see was the cotton gin strap hitting my outstretched hand or my buttock as it was stuck through the back of a folding chair. They would witness my character and spirit being physically wrecked with each stroke. After several years of these beatings, I wanted so badly to just give up, quit school and become just another sharecropper. However, I knew this would break Mom's heart as well as disrespect my ancestors. Second grade continued to be a struggle for me as many other strange and harsh things happened.

Asphidity bag

During the Polio era of 1955, as a second grader, God became more real to me. It was a late fall evening after school when some of the older boys in our community tried to instigate fights between boys my age, as usual. That day, they tried to instigate a fight between myself and Buddy, who was a victim of polio and had to wear leg braces. As they egged Buddy on to fight me and he came limping and swinging at me, I was unable to hit him. Each time I attempted to throw a punch at him, I lost all strength and power in my right arm and fist. Initially, I thought it had something to do with that awful-smelling bag I had to wear around my neck for polio pre-vention. Later on in life, I learned that it was God who had prevented me from punching or hitting Buddy, not that Asphidity bag.

Many African Americans, including my Mom, used Asphidity bags, and we all had to wear one tied to a string hanging around our neck. I can barely remember wearing the bag or the awful smell; however, to Mom, not wearing the bag meant contracting polio. The wisdom of the older generation was not to be questioned. You simply did what you were told to do because your elders believed and knew that home remedies worked. I did not have a choice in wearing the bag. That little smelly bag provided all the faith and hope Mom needed against us getting polio.

The Catch

Spring of 1955, I saw my brother Willie make one of the greatest catches I had ever seen while playing center field for Montgomery High School. The batter rocketed the next pitch to deep centerfield. At that time, our athletic department did not have the money to purchase baseball cleats so Willie chased down that rocket fly ball wearing his regular shoes. He overran it, and as he was trying to make the catch, his feet slipped from underneath him and while falling to the ground on his back, he made the catch. The runner on third started home, but then realized that Willie had made the catch. As the runner was returning to third, Willie got up and rifled a deadly throw to the third baseman for the out, a double play. The small crowd cheered wildly. From that day on, I wanted to be a baseball player like Willie.

Uncle JD was one of the greatest first basemen in his time. His motto was that "my infielders could throw a baseball too high for him to catch but never too low for him to pick it." Each time he stepped on the diamond, he proved it with his stylish stretches of digging the baseball out of the dirt when it was thrown low onto the ground.

As for Sim, he was really Mr. Cool on the basketball court. He displayed one of the most consistent, accurate fade away jump shots of his time. The only person who could give him some competition was one of his teammates, whom we called "Boy-Blue," James Allen Toom. He would later become my basketball mentor.

Of course, helping mom all those years deprived me of valuable practice time, making my chances of being a good athlete look very slim. To achieve those guys' greatness seemed impossible. They were really special athletes. I had spent ninety percent of my time with Mom and Grandma and being "Water Boy" for those who worked the cotton fields, which left my athletic skills undeveloped. Therefore, when it came time for picking teams for any sport, you can guess where my stock or team popularity was; let's just say "not first" and leave it there for now. The next year, I worked diligently on improving my athletic skills by using all the free time I had after completing daily chores around the house and my "Water Boy" responsibilities. As my second year of school came to a close the only thing I had to look forward to was those...cotton fields.

My Clorox Bleach episode

Late in August of 1955, after playing outside I was very thirty so I went in the house to find something to drink. Once in the kitchen, I saw this clear liquid in a glass sitting on the kitchen table and thought that it was a Bubble Up soda and wanted to drink it before anyone else got it. So after I took a big swallow of it I realized that it wasn't Bubble Up soda nor water. Once that liquid entered my mouth and I had swallowed some of it, I knew that I was in serious trouble. Within seconds of swallowing it, my whole insides felt like they were on fire, just like my hands felt when I played Wile E. Coyote cowboy. Everything I had eaten was now coming up as I experienced one of the worst tastes ever. I cried out for Mom and she came running, asking what was wrong, and I told her I had drunk some of what was in the glass on the table. She told me that I had swallowed some Clorox bleach. She immediately called for the old reliable bottle of castor oil. And she gave me a big dose of it. I was sick for days. She repeated the castor oil dosage until I was able to eat solid food again. I don't know what was worse, drinking that bleach or taking castor oil for days!

September 1956...

As a third grader, on one of those hot and steamy days after eating my greasy brown-bag lunch, that consisted of fried sweet potatoes, Mom's delicious homemade biscuits with some cold salt pork from supper between them, I was having a great time playing with the other kids and different kinds of games, in particular riding on the merry-go-round that was turning so fast I had to hang on for dear life with all my might to keep from being thrown off. This made me dizzy, and I was really thirsty after eating that salty pork and waiting in line at the drinking fountain. When it came to my turn, I drank a great deal of water, went back to class and got out my reading book in preparation for my reading class, which I was not looking forward to. However, our reading teacher had to attend a meeting at the principal's office. This gave me some relief, but she left one of her favorite students in charge to write down the names of any students who talked, got out of their seat or did not read silently.

In her absence, there were several students, of course, out of their seats and a couple of boys sitting in back of me who were talking. As usual, I was quiet, pretending to be reading, but mostly looking at the pictures since I could not read at the time. I did not want to bring any attention to myself for fear of being called on to read out loud once she returned, which is still a big fear of mine to this day! When our teacher returned from her meeting, she received the list. Unbeknown to me, my name was on her list for talking, and there was no debating the list or its consequences. Her consequences for that day for your name being on it were that you had to remain indoors during recess. This meant I could not go outside to play, eliminating any possible chances of using the bathroom. To say the least, I was very upset for a couple of reasons. Number 1 being I was not talking and was being punished for something I did not do. Number 2 being I did not understand nor could I question why my name was on that list.

My anger began to kick in, even though I was afraid to say anything or ask to use the bathroom. About fifteen minutes before dismissal time at 3:00 p.m. I had to use the bathroom very, very badly after drinking all that water at lunch. I thought I had only one option, which was to hold it until school was out at 3:00 p.m. then make a mad dash to the bathroom before boarding Big Yellow. The other option was too embarrassing to consider, but it happened.

Now in my attempt to deceive my soon-to-be school bus (Big Yellow) audience, I sat quietly in my seat and waited until my classmates had left the room hoping that no one would recognize that I had wet my pants. Once outside of the classroom, in my attempt to continue the cover up of this most unfortunate and embarrassing incident, I quickly went to that same water fountain at the end of the hallway by the front doors where earlier I had drank my fill after recess. I quickly put water over the sides of my pants; the front and back were already wet. I headed outside to the playground, started rolling around in the dirt pretending to be playing Cowboys and Indians. This was the way I hoped to trick everyone on "Big Yellow." Pretty ingenious, huh?

Once on the bus, for that four-mile ride home, the older students and some of my peers starting asking why my pants were so wet and dirty. I told them that I was hot and poured water on myself to cool off and then I went to play while waiting for our bus to arrive. However, my attempt to mislead my fellow riders had failed horribly and this embarrassing moment would linger with me all summer and into the 4th grade. Some of my classmates teased me by calling me "pee boy," but they later stopped for whatever reasons. Maybe my older brothers or my sister, the enforcer, had something to say to them.

As I look back on that incident, I realize that it affected me both mentally and physically, as well as positively and negatively. It taught me that no disciplinary action of any kind that any teacher could dish out should be worth the emotional and psychological embarrassment this incident had caused me. And that no other person has the right to place any of God's children in such a compromising position as the one I had to endure. This incident and the a.k.a. corporal punishment days certainly shaped my approach to my future career.

This type of embarrassment could and probably has scarred some children for life. The positive side to this dreadful example of disciplinary tactics, if there is one, is that if this autobiography is ever published, any adolescent can see that with God's help they can recover from anything!

Chapter 7

TRYING TIMES...

I N THE FALL OF 1957, I was retained and had to repeat the fourth grade for the second time. It would prove to be a trying time in my life. I had to regain my self-respect and change the ways that most of my new classmates and a few acquaintances had responded toward me since that embarrassing wetting my pants incident. I also wanted to get back the attention from those older girls who would always pinch my cheeks and make remarks about how cute I was. Each time I boarded or exited the Big Yellow, I believed that the only way to regain my peer self-respect and that popularity with the older girls was to become a sports legend like my brothers, Willie and Sim, or Boy Blue! Little did I know at the time that the popularity I so desperately wanted from those older girls would turn into another devastating incident in my life!

To achieve Willie, Sim and Boy Blue's successes and greatness in the games I had grown to love, I had to work very hard at developing my basketball and baseball athletic skills. In addition, I had to improve my grades so I would be eligible to compete for a starting position my sophomore, junior, then senior years in high school. To start these new challenges of mine, I needed a place to practice and better ways to study. Academics were always a concern of mine, but my main focus or challenge was first to improve my athletic skills. There was no one my age or any friends to practice with, and even if there were, there were no basketball courts or baseball fields within miles of my house. What was I to do? I had no choice but to focus on basketball, because in our community that was the only sport that one could practice unaccompanied.

Using the available space behind our house, I began to construct my homemade basketball court. I developed a hoop out of a wire clothes hanger and nailed it to the back of our house by its hook and stem. Then I bent the body of the hanger downwards to extend it away from the house and pulled it open to make a round hoop. Now I had my backboard and hoop and our backyard became the basketball court.

My next dilemma was to construct a basketball that would be compatible in weight and size to my wire hanger hoop. Since a real basketball would be too large in weight and size, I asked myself where or how I could get my hands on such a basketball that would fit my need. I knew for sure that no one was going to give me one. I was then left with only one other option; I had to somehow make myself a basketball.

Secret Missions

To do this I had to undertake two secret missions. First, I had to snatch one of Mom's stockings without her knowing. Secondly, I had to harvest some cotton from the field behind our house without Mom or the Big Boss man discovering it. Late one horribly humid afternoon, I snuck deep into the cotton field behind our house and picked some of the puffiest cotton to build my homemade basketball. By stuffing it into the stocking that I had commandeered from Mom, I formed a well-rounded replica of a basketball just about the right size for my homemade hoop. My ingenuity prevailed as I now had a hoop, basketball and backboard, all created by me!

With my homemade stocking basketball, each chance I got, I was outside playing on my basketball court in back of our house and with a featherweight ball that couldn't be dribbled I had to simply imagine dribbling around players for a layup, or stopping to take that last second jump shot to win a game! This became an obsession for me. It took the place of food, other games, acquaintances and house chores, etc. If anyone was looking for me, they knew just where they could find me – on my homemade court, doing my thing; playing the game I hoped would eventually change our lives for the better. All my practice made things that much easier for me once I got onto a real court with a real ball. Even though Mom knew I took one of her stockings and filled it with cotton to make a basketball, she never mentioned it or how she felt about it. Looking back now, I can't believe she didn't punish; obviously, buying new stockings would rarely be in the budget!

On a real court, naturally, there was much more maneuvering space behind the backboard, especially doing lay-up drills or while driving to the basket for a slam-dunk. And best of all, there would be no back of the house to crash into. Wow! I was playing basketball now. From an early age, I was taught to always believe in God and Christ and there was a destiny for everyone; that good and bad things happen in one's life, and there is a reason why. That's why it is so important to recognize God and Christ in good times as well as in bad times.

Speaking of good times, Mom had started a new job as a cook at this place called the Roadhouse, a whites-only bar across the highway from our house. How convenient for her; now she would not have to walk miles to work at that plantation owner's house. Plus, things had just begun to start to get better for us with the extra money she was earning.

The Roadhouse

Although the Roadhouse was segregated, the main group was hunters who came from all parts of Mississippi and as far away as Arkansas and Tennessee to go deer hunting in the woods in back of our house and surrounding communities. They came in droves, and deer would sometimes be right by our house. These deer hunters would stop at the Roadhouse to get something to eat and drink and to feed their horses before and after their hunts. They had some of the most beautiful horses and horse trailers and all kind of guns with scopes on them. This also was a time of great concern by Mom for our safety with those hunters so close to our house. She insisted that I stay in our yard when playing outside and away from the cotton fields. She wanted to make sure the hunters didn't mistake me for a deer while I was playing cowboys and Indians in the cotton fields in back of our house.

Christmas Morning & Fire Crackers

However, a devastating event did take place at the Roadhouse on that brisk, windy, Christmas morning of 1957 that would change our lives for a long time. As I was outside playing cowboys and Indians, wearing my two new holsters and cap pistols that I had gotten from Santa Claus (which was very rare that we would get new toys), I saw the son of the bar owner, who seemed to be a few years older than me, outside shooting off some fire-crackers. We had never met nor played with one another; and I thank God that we hadn't befriended because of the awful incident that occurred that morning. I can imagine what would have happened to me if I had been connected or involved in that firecracker shooting incident. I saw him shooting off some firecrackers and he seemed to be having so much fun. This made me wish that I had some firecrackers to shoot, as well. However, without warning that brisk southwestern wind quickly changed direction and starting blowing straight toward the Roadhouse. From my position in our front yard, it seemed to me that he still had a large sum of firecrackers yet to light but only a few matches remaining. I watched intensively and waited with curiosity as he thought through his option of how he was going to light the remaining fire crackers when he had gotten to his last match.

When he did finally get to that last match, and in his attempt to keep a fire going, he began to gather dried grass and sticks to build a fire with that last match. He didn't seem to have any concern for how hard that wind had started to blow toward his father's bar as he struck that last match and lit his makeshift campfire of piled grass, twigs and sticks. The wind suddenly picked up and blew his makeshift fire into the other dry grass. Can you guess where it headed next? Yep, that fire headed straight for the Roadhouse; suddenly, he started screaming and calling for his father.

"Father, father!" he was yelling. "Come quickly!" He then ran toward the front door of the Roadhouse, still yelling for his father. Finally, his father came running out and saw that the fire his son had started was heading straight for his bar, burning out of control. Now! Neither our neighborhood of Anchor Curve nor the town of Louise, four miles away, had fire departments! The nearest fire department was in Yazoo City, about fourteen miles away.

In the owner's frantic attempts to extinguish the fire by using a bucket to carry water from inside the bar to the fire failed. The owner then took his frustrations out on his son by beating him over the head and body with that very same bucket. The owner's son was just standing there crying with blood streaming down the side of his head and face. By the time the Yazoo City fire department arrived, the Roadhouse was smoldering ashes!

That Christmas morning that started out filled with joy had quickly turned to one filled with sadness and devastation for all of us – the owner, his son, the deer hunters, Mom and our entire family. We all had suffered a great loss that day! I assume the greatest loss was for the owner and his son. Even though we were never friends, nor even talked to each other, I felt really terrible for him and his father for the way things happened to them on that Christmas morning in 1957. I was sorrier for Mom and the rest of us because I thought that the fire had destroyed another opportunity for us to have a better life.

Chapter 8

A BLESSING FOLLOWS DEVASTATION...

As the heat of the 1957 summer ended along with the burning down of the Roadhouse, I was blessed with a place to perfect my basketball skills, right in front of our house: the old Roadhouse spot. Once the owner had salvaged what he wanted, underneath the remaining rubbish was a slab of concrete that I thought had "Joe's basketball court" written all over it, but that was short lived. My brother Sim, Boy Blue and their friends took advantage of that space to build their basketball court. While my brother and his friends were cleaning up the rubbish, I lurked nearby and found melted nickels, dimes and quarters from the cash register and the slot machines and a few of them salvageable, so all was not lost for me. They built a backboard, attached a real basketball hoop to it and fastened it to a huge telephone pole that seem to be eleven feet tall. Dug a hole about foot or so deep and planted that pole in it. They were now in the basketball-playing business.

All was not lost for me, even though I had lost what I thought was a blessing for me. I could now watch my brother and his friends play hoops, basketball, and if they were short a player, they would use me as their substitute, a whipping boy or offer me up as a sacrificial lamb. What a joy it was to play with those guys, even though most of the time they would school me, making me look really stupid, but I was still learning to play the game that I had grown to love from the best players. Those were the times I treasured the most that summer.

With the kind of weather we had in the Deep South, I could play hoops with my brother, my mentor Boy Blue and their friends almost year round. Too bad that during this time, northern or southern colleges and university recruiters did not recognize the talent of our small town black athletes. Of course, the educating of Joe on the basketball court was not the only education I received at that time that would change my life for years to come. My basketball education and academics, like all sharecroppers' kids, had to take a back seat to our daily ritual of sharecropping duties during spring cultivation in late April, May and early June. And fall harvesting in October, November and into December kept me busy. What extra time I did have I tried to use it to perfect my athletic skills and get my homework done so I could be eligible for basketball tryouts in my freshman year.

My Other Private Education

It took place on one of those humid early fall weekend days in 1959 on the front porch and ended hours later in the hot and steamy cornfields out back of the Big House.

My brother Sim; my sister, Lueretha; my uncle JD; my cousin William; his girlfriend; and some of their friends were having an intimate, heated conversation. I was sitting on the bike of my best friend Al by the front porch while holding on to a fifty gallon barrel used for catching rainwater. I was pretending to be riding his bike even though I didn't know how to ride a bike at that time in my life. Their conversation mostly focused on sex and they were using words they thought I wouldn't understand, which led to the conception of one of my second cousins. It all seemed to be harmless, and they were just having fun as usual. As soon as Mom came from the kitchen calling for me, that conversation ceased and one of a less intense tone took its place. I thought Mom wanted me to help her with some kitchen chores or she wanted to get me away from around them, thinking they would be annoyed with someone as young as me hanging around. Or maybe she thought that I might hear or learn something that would corrupt her innocent son. Little did she know the chore she was about to send me on would do just that.

The errand Mom had for me to do was to go and harvest some corn for supper. This involved taking a corn sack and trekking to the cornfield to pull some ears of corn. Her intent was to take me away from gossip far more interesting than that of tearing off some ears of corn. Quite naturally, I wasn't pleased to leave a conversation about the birds and the bees, so to speak.

After all, it was an 11-year-old's perfect opportunity to get some tips on how to respond to those older girls who would always call me cute and pinch my cheek as I entered or exited Big Yellow. After I had gotten the corn

sack and had started to walk toward the cornfield approximately fifty yards in back of the Big House, one of my
sister's friends called to me. "Skeeter," she said. "Wait
for me. I want to help you pull the ears of corn so it won't
take you so long." Once she caught up with me, she said,
"I know you didn't want to leave our conversation and
what did you think of it?"

Not knowing just what to say at the time and trying so
desperately to be cool, as I was scared to death and didn't
want to make a fool of myself, I replied, "It seemed okay,
I guess." Once we were inside the cornfield and out of
sight of the Big House and the others, she asked me if I
knew what they were really talking about. Still worried
about not looking stupid in the eyes of such a beautiful
girl, who I thought only wanted to help me pull some ears
of corn, I answered, "Yes! Sex!" I thought this was my
lucky day. She was going to fill me in on what the gossip
was really about. How lucky I was to have such a beautiful girl finish the conversation with me.

Little did I know she wanted to do more than pull
some ears of corn and complete a conversation that sweltering summer afternoon in our cornfield! As we began to
pull ears of corn, she moved closer to me, standing by my
side and then she placed her arm around my shoulder. It
didn't seem real, being touched by her soft, warm hand.
My heart rate suddenly rocketed to a thousand times a
second! I was frozen in time, not knowing what was
going to happen next. Without any words being spoken,
she slowly shifted her position to the front of me with
both hands resting on my shoulder, as if it were her privilege for a dance.

The next thought that came to my mind was what would happen if I ran in protest or fear? What would she think of me? I just fixated on the stalks behind her. As badly as my body wanted to, I was unwilling to bring myself to look her in the eyes or hug her. Casually, she moved even closer and slid her hands from my shoulder to my waist while I trembled nervously. Now our bodies touched as her hand moved to the front of my short pants. I could hear insects, frogs and grasshoppers begging for a cool breeze or rain to cool us both off.

As she told me to "lie down," I was filled with fear. Her voice now did not sound the same as it did when she was on the porch. It was mysterious as she pressed me back on to the ground. Hastily, she moved me on top of her. She was making strange, rapid, soft breathing sounds while undoing my pants as she moved back and forth under me. I thought that Mom or someone would come looking for me to save or remove me from this inescapable moment in time.

She finally had my pants down and she pulled me into her, which delivered a warm and somewhat pleasurable pain. She moved her hips in a circular motion under me and instructed me to do the same movements in a voice of soft overtones different from any I had ever heard before. I can't say for sure how long this encounter lasted but it left me bruised and sore for what seemed like weeks. Her next words were that she better go back now and join the others, and she warned me not to say anything about this, and if she hurt me, she was sorry.

For months, I felt sullied and in a state of fright and disbelief, not knowing what to do or say to Mom or anyone about what had happened to me. For many years

111

to come, that encounter placed an inexhaustible fear upon me of older girls and young women. It was to the point that many of my friends would tease me and ask me if I was a "faggot" (an unfortunate term then and now), due to my reluctance to engage in those extracurricular activities they were more than willing to get involved in.

Chapter 9

-1959 COMPLEXITY-

Over the next eight years or so, following my first sexual encounter, were some of the most trying times for me. Mom would remarry and we had to move to another one of Mr. Lawrence's plantations; this one bordered Mr. Hudy Montgomery's land on the northeast side of the big city of Louise. My three older brothers, Sam, Willie and Sim, had already moved to Greenville, Mississippi, to start carving out their future. At first, I thought the only good thing that could come from this move was that I would be in walking distance to Louise and away from the memories of my cornfield episode.

This also was a time when my generation, especially my older brothers and their friends, began to take offense to the tactics, working conditions and low wages of sharecropping. When sharecroppers' children, especially sons around seventeen or eighteen, began to take offense to the rules of the plantation owners, their parents would ship them away to live with relatives in the northern cities, usually Chicago, in fear for their safety if not for their lives. The fear of relationships developing between the black males and white females, even of a platonic nature, were strictly forbidden. However, none of the women that were black or biracial were forbidden fruit to the white males. He could take his liberty with any female fruit, ripe or not, he deemed his, without any repercussions. For the black male, it was the garden of the forbidden fruit of any relationship, especially if the white males were picking fruit from that same garden!

For example there were a couple biracial young ladies in our communities who white males had formed relationships with that led to two heinous murders. Eddy Davis Jr., an 18-year-old black male and friend to my brother Sim, suffered a gruesome slaying and had his body dragged through a small village to his parents' home one Saturday night in 1960. They lived less than three miles from our house. Eddy Senior was our "Big Yellow" driver. Eddy Jr.'s crime was that he allegedly had been dating a biracial girl that was in a relationship with a white male.

Then there was the lynching of a one-armed black man, Rainy Pool, in 1962 on the railroad tracks near our house north of Louise. He had forbidden his daughter to continue a relationship with a white male. Of course, at that time I was afraid to even speak of these incidents let alone write of them. However, it was alleged that Mr. Pool had been out drinking the night he met his hangmen, his executioners. They had a story about his murder in Jet magazine.

Also during this time, from 1961 into 1962, mass arrests and violence were touched off when Freedom Riders, actively seeking to spur integration, made

Mississippi a major target. There was not even a token integration in our public schools, let alone in the state of Mississippi schools and colleges, until 1962 when the state of Mississippi government failed unsuccessfully to block the admission of James H. Meredith, an African American, to the University of Mississippi law school.

With the unrest about education in our state at that time, plantation owners finally gave in to the compulsory law in the fall of 1962 that required all children under the age of 16 to attend school. This truly was one of the happiest days of my life! I could now finally go to school each day and not be forced to work in those horrible cotton fields any longer during school hours. I thought, at least we had won the battle against the cruelty of slavery that evolved to sharecropping that left so many uneducated people in its path of destruction.

However, racial antagonisms continued and resulted in many more acts of violence: Churches and homes were bombed. Violence continued in the early morning of June 12, 1963, just hours after President John F. Kennedy delivered his speech on national television in support of civil rights movement. Medgar Willey Evers had just pulled into his driveway after returning from a meeting with NAACP lawyers. As he emerged from his car and carrying NAACP T-shirts that read "Jim Crow Must Go," "evil prevail again," Evers was struck in the back with a bullet fired from an Enfield 1917 rifle that ricocheted into his house. He would later perish at a local hospital. Also during that time, three civil-rights workers (two white, one black) were murdered the next year; and there were many less publicized outrages. With all the mayhem the south was experiencing, especially in our and surrounding communities with the two murders and the KKK on the prowl, I began to understand why Mom forbade me from being with her to keep me from forming friendships with plantation owners' kids. She had foreseen the possible dangers that could have come from me developing a friendship with her employer's son, and especially his daughter.

After those two horrific murders in our community, the Freedom Riders came to Louise, Mississippi, in July 1963. Their march brought them less than 200 yards from our home en route to their encampment at Mr. Hudy Montgomery's estate. It was exciting to have the Freedom Riders come to our neighborhood and so close to our house, but it was also disappointing because Mom forbid us to attend any of the rallies! She was afraid of the consequences that could come from being associated with the Freedom Riders.

She said, "We still have to live here and try to make a living after they have left." Being known as this quiet, level-headed and nonviolent person, people around me didn't know just how angry I was inside at all the social injustices plaguing our race and communities. These incidents of murders and not being able to attend the Freedom Rider's rallies angered me so much that I was looking for things to reach out in anger against to strike a blow in violence. Then I would remember Dr. King's words and belief of nonviolence and his famous speech: "**I Have a Dream**... *Let us not seek to satisfy our thirst for freedom by drinking from the cup of bitterness and hatred. We must practice nonviolence. That one day this nation will rise up and live out the true meaning of its creed: We hold these truths to be self-evident: that all men are created* *equal. Also, that our children will one day live in a nation where they will not be judged by the color of their skin, but by the content of their character..."*

Being born and raised in a small town in the heart of the Delta, there is an entirely different attitude held as far as the right norms and values instilled in someone. I believed and understood what Dr. King meant about *"having a dream that one day even the state of Mississippi, a desert state, sweltering with the heat of injustice and oppression, will be transformed into an oasis of freedom and justice."* So I would ask myself, would I live to see it?

I have seen and experienced many changes because of Dr. King's dream, but the dream has not yet fully materialized. That day is still to come, because so many are still living in poverty in this country. Even today, for many, the persistence of racial conflicts, low wages and forced labor that I experienced through the 50s and 60s in Mississippi as a child, teenager and young adult still exists in many states, countries and nations today with the sole purpose to feed another's greed!

It seemed that I would never be able escape greed and all its excessive desires that were placed on being successful after moving to our new community on the northwest side. We were still sharecroppers experiencing the rigid backbreaking work, low-to-no wages, but the abbreviated school attendance would be ending with enforcement of the compulsory law. But most importantly Mom seemed to be finally happy. I was now in need of another mentor since we moved and Sim moved to Greenville, Mississippi, and Boy Blue off to college.

Maybe it could be Jerry, my new brother, who had a semi-rim makeshift basketball court in the front yard that consisted of a small bicycle rim nailed to a wooden backboard and attached to a pole approximately eight feet high on the side of the garage. It was not to be after I learned that one of my new neighbors, Roy Jones, had a state-of-the-art, regulation basketball court with a real hoop and net in his front yard and he played on the varsity basketball team for the Montgomery Wolverines. Roy's house was also where history was made in our community because of when the Freedom Riders encamped on Mr. Hudy Montgomery's land they had to travel on the road behind Roy's house.

Now my only problem was grade improvement and becoming acclimated to my new family. Mom's new husband already had six children, three girls and three boys, and his father lived with him, too. This with the five of us and the elder lady, Ms. P. Ross, who occupied the other side of the duplex where we lived at Anchor Curve, who Mom cared for, made a family of thirteen; nine children and five adults living in a four-bedroom house.

For the first year, even with the overcrowding, things seemed to be going well for Mom, my two new brothers and me, with the exception of school! I was still having some problems with my grades that I needed to correct. However, I could sense some discomfort coming from my sister Lueretha, not necessarily because of the rules of the house or her chores. I didn't know if it was something personal or not, but I knew that she wouldn't be living with us much longer before she would strike out on her own. I just did what I was told to do and kept to myself. I tried to stay away from the house as much as possible by playing basketball at Roy's house. What an opportunity that was for me to be able to play with Roy and his friends. When I did have to be home, I tried to do things that would keep me outside and to myself. I played basketball on our semi-rim makeshift court or sat watching the clouds, daydreaming of things I wanted to accomplish in life. Sometimes I would pretend to be Willie making that great catch. I would throw up clods of dirt or rocks into the air and catch them as I was falling to the ground on my back. Or I would then smash them with a broomstick for homeruns as I would go into my make-believe homerun jog of the winning run.

Then it was back to reality as the eldest son of Mom's husband's problems finally caused him to move to Chicago to live with his older sister. This seemed to ease some of the tension in the house. However, there was always some tension between Mom's husband and his next oldest son and daughter, as well as with my sister. I had my suspicions as to why there was so much anxiety between my sister and him. I also knew why there was this tension between him and his children. They remembered how their mother had been treated by this man before she passed away. And thanks to God, they did not take it out on Mom. That house was beginning to turn into a house of pain, and everyone was leaving when they got a chance.

Speaking of Leaving!!!

On one of those unusually hot Sundays in January of 1964, I was at Roy's house after a week's work for our usual Sunday afternoon basketball game with the guys when I saw my sister coming. I knew that something was dreadfully wrong. She would never come to Roy's home unless something was wrong due to some kind of a rivalry between her and Roy's sister. Contemplating what I had done wrong, I grilled myself to see if I had failed to complete all my chores. No! It must be something of a more serious or important nature than my chores for her to come and get me. Could it be something awful had happened between Mom and her husband? Whatever it was, my basketball time would end that day. As she came closer to us, I could see from the expression on her face that something was seriously wrong. She walked up to me and looked me in the eyes and said that Mom wanted me home because grandmother Retta had taken sick en route to her cousin's funeral and had to be rushed to the hospital in Yazoo City. We hurried home in order to go back to Anchor Curve to see what was wrong with my beloved Grandma Retta.

Upon arriving at Anchor Curve, Mom and other relatives went to her bedside in the hospital in Yazoo City. Grandmother Retta had an undetected brain aneurysm. The doctors told them that a vein in her head had burst and they could not fix it. The only thing they could do for her was to try to make her as comfortable as possible.

Later on that week, her health started to turn for the worse and she had to be moved to a more modern hospital in Greenville, Mississippi, to make her more relaxed. We all knew that in that era, medical personnel, especially in the Deep South, were not equipped to handle an illness like hers. Everyone was very concerned, sad and worried about Grandma Retta because she wasn't a sickly lady, even after giving birth to twelve children. This was the first time that I had experienced a serious but deadly sickness in our family.

At that time in my life I was afraid of the dead, and I would never see her again on earth. Grandma knew that I was afraid of the dead because I had lived with her most of my life in Anchor Curve before moving to Louise, and she knew that it was her time to go and be with God. So Grandma sent word to us to not be afraid of her, because she would never do anything to harm us.

On Friday, January 24, 1964, Grandma Retta Smith-Fountain went home to be with God. We said our final goodbyes at her funeral on February 8, 1964. What a loss to our family; she was its backbone. Just fourteen years later, Grandpa Lem went home also to be with God August 1978.

I WAS A FRESHMAN in high school in 1963-1964 and what a year! It all began with many difficulties as I was trying to adjust to my new surroundings while being the oldest student in class. I was terrified by the misery of Corporal Punishment days, the sophomore, junior and senior girls, as well as girls in my grade. And the loss of my Grandma only added to my pain and misery. I had no one I could talk to about all the hurt I was experiencing as I tried to find my place among such a young and imma-ture group of freshmen. Even the undeveloped group of freshmen seemed to have less difficulty in finding their place or social groups than I did. Of course, I did not initially fit into any of my classmates' social groups at that time; gratefully, later on I did. I had no idea about nor had anyone prepared me for the difficulties I had to face as a freshmen or throughout high school. I titled my freshman year as my "Losing Season." There was little or no encouragement from anyone, except for Roy, who would say, "You can do this! Hang in there, Skeeter!"

I concluded that there was no encouragement from anyone else because no one could have known just how difficult life was for me at that time. I had the appearance of being this quiet older teen who was afraid of girls for whatever reasons. Plus, I couldn't read and write to save my life and thought that basketball could possibly save me from becoming just another crofter. At the time, I could not understand why my academic achievement and personal life were so different from other students, but I knew one thing for sure: I was not going to let anything or anyone stop me from finishing high school, no matter what or how long it took.

I wanted to go to college as much as Mom wanted me to go to college. I would pray to God that when I grew up and had children, they would not be raised in an uneducated, fractured environment or community. They would be nurtured by me, and I would make sure they had nice things and a chance to attend any college or university of their choice. And with God's help, I have been able to keep that promise.

Now! By no means am I saying that Mom did not do an outstanding job in taking care of me and my brothers and sister with what she had to work with, because she did an exceptional job. She was a mother, father and a saint all rolled up into one in her children's eyes and many others.

Even the game that I had grown to love so much over the years, and which caused me to spend countless hours in the blazing hot sun working hard to improve my skills, I now thought had started to fail me.

Coach Woolfolk's Starting Five...

In order for me to break into Coach Woolfolk's starting five of Adam, Dee, Chatman, Roy, and Melvin (who unfortunately later died in the Vietnam War), I had to be just as good or better than my mentors. I had to accept that those five guys were the best athletes on the team at the time and gave us the best chance to win a championship for now. I was satisfied with that because my brother and mentors had taught me, as well as showed me, that team play is much better than individual honor. That's why it was called a "TEAM"– whether it was a basketball TEAM, a baseball TEAM or a football TEAM. They all symbolize the TEAM spirit as one. So even though I didn't like it, I sat and cheered for them. I even went as far as to share with Adam my new Converse gym shoes that I had worked hard all summer to earn enough money to buy for the start of the new season. All of this to show TEAM spirit and togetherness. Right!

After all the preparations, anticipation and watching various moves players would make to either free them-selves for shots or draw their defenders to them to free up teammates' shots, I would go outside on the court and try to imitate or mimic all their moves. I believed that even though I was a freshman I would be ready to step in and play. After all, I was the same age as many of my team-mates but just not in the same grade. However, I still had to sit and watch them play. As I sat and watched, I often wondered what other surprises life might have in store for me. Maybe those teachers and other individuals were right that I would never amount to anything; just another sharecropper, like family members before me, a Nobody.

Even though I was not starting in my freshmen year, I was fortunate to still be on the team. And with Chatman and Dee being seniors, there was hope for me to break into the starting lineup my sophomore year. Just by being on the team, I could see that coach Woolfolk had some confidence in my basketball skills. I would use our warm-up drills before each game to showcase my jumping, shooting and ball control abilities, just as we used our figure eight lay-up drills to really get the crowd going.

Getting Everyone Fired Up

It was controlled chaos! The girls would be singing, dancing, shouting out their cheers; the football players would be pounding and stomping their feet on the bleachers; Damon, our star running back, the score clock operator, would be standing on top of the scorer table talking trash. Coach Woolfolk would be walking the side-line with his line-up and play sheets rolled up in his right hand with this look on his face "Boy, you better not... this up," especially when we played our rival Belzoni high school, approximately twelve miles north of Louise. I just sat there, watched and waited for my turn and took in all I could to prepare for my chance that hopefully would come soon. Coach Woolfolk's starters, the upper classmen, all had girlfriends; some were dating seriously and planned on getting married after graduation. At that time, I had only a few close friends who I would hang out with at school during lunch, in study hall or during P.E. classes. As strange as it may seem based on my trau-matic cornfield experience when I was 11, most of my friends ended up being girls. One of my best friends then was Elnora, the star player for the girls' team, the Montgomery Wolverettes. She could single-handedly take a game over and lead her team to a victory. What a player she was, as were the other Lady Wolverines, like Sadie, Dorothy Earl, Ernestine and Helen.

The Fall of 1965

My sophomore year, two small local segregated middle schools or junior high schools (Midnight and Silver City) were rezoned to be part of the Humphrey County School District. Among those students were outstanding basketball, football and baseball players who wouldn't now attend Belzoni High school; they had to attend Montgomery High School. That made us one of the powerhouse schools in our conference, and I was the starting center on the basketball team, the starting wide receiver on the football team and the first baseman on the baseball team. It seemed at last that all the hard work had begun to pay off. We were now winning games and competing for championships, with the exception of football.

The girls were winning, as well, with the addition of Ernestine and a powerful lefty to the already outstanding Elnora, Helen and Dorothy Earl, with Sadie graduating. Both girls and boys teams were winning games that no one but we thought we could win. School was now good academically and personally. I had great friends and teammates. What more could I ask for, right?

Little did I know that the merger of the Midnight and Sliver City schools would cause such serious conflicts! I felt that each student should be openly accepted, not just the female athletes or male jocks. I must have thought I was living in some kind of mystical cocoon to think that could happen. I failed to realize that dating back farther than my brothers' and Boy Blue's days to that present

High School Friend

time, when it came to rivalries, humans are creatures of habit. This fierce competition involved more than defending ones' scholastic ability; it involved defending one's integrity of manhood and womanhood.

With the arrival of all the new boys and girls, it was like the California's Gold Rush. Everyone was staking their claim and was willing to go to any measure to protect it. After a couple of months, I thought things had cooled down and the gold rush was over. So I began to befriend some of the transfer students, both guys and girls. I, along with one of my friends, Robert Davis, the starting full-back on the football team (brother of Eddy Davis Jr. who was murdered), were the first ones to openly cross the line and date girls who transferred in from Midnight or Silver City. We did not know that earlier in the week several guys from Montgomery and some of the guys from Midnight and Silver City had an altercation; no major fistfight, just some trash talking and physical posturing between them over who was dating whom. Two of my close friends from the football team, Booker T. and Cleo, were involved in that dispute, causing serious problems for me since I had friends on both sides of that difference of opinion.

This clash put me in the middle, but I chose not to take sides. I only intervened in an attempt to try and stop it before it escalated, but it came to blows between me and Cleo that next morning. As I was getting off Big Yellow, he walked up to me and punched me in the chest and called me a traitor. I immediately went after him to retaliate. As several teachers were coming outside to supervise the arrival of the buses, they quickly defused the incident from escalating. Cooler heads prevailed and continued to do so after a stern lecture by Coach Woolfolk in regards to not playing sports again if it continued. And his sister, Mrs. Bennett, our English teacher, and math instructor, Mr. Wheeler, warned us in regards to not graduating if this conflict did not cease. We all chose the latter and felt that friendship and graduation were more important than feuding!

Chapter 10

MY SUMMER VACATION OF 1966...!

The summer of 1966 and throughout that upcoming school year, it was filled with a mixture of life-shaping experiences and adventures! It started with my summer vacation that I spent with my brother Sim, and his family on the Westside of Chicago! Just a few blocks from of the heart of its notorious ghetto. Not aware of what that city had in store for me, I was just glad I was out of Mississippi and not working in the hot cotton and soybean fields that summer. And to have some time to unwind from my sophomore losing season and the rivalry that came along with rezoning of Silver City and Midnight schools that I had mistakenly assumed would be great. And I needed to rethink what I could do to prepare for my upcoming junior year. Although I was saddened to leave Mom, my two brothers, new girlfriend (Wilma), my close platonic girlfriends and others behind, even if it was only for a couple of months. Wilma, a very beautiful and lovely girl, and I had planned to have a serious relationship once I returned from vacation. My anticipation to see this city "Chicago" that everyone raved about with such enthusiasm outweighed me leaving all my loved ones behind. Therefore, my Greyhound bus trip to Chicago seemed long and tiresome with anticipation. I was a nervous traveler, filled with expectation like a child wanting to know that age old question, "are we there yet?" especially when we arrived in Effingham, Illinois, for our first extended rest stop. To this Delta teen, Effingham seemed huge compared to Louise! In reality, Chicago was at least 100 times larger.

With our Greyhound bus finally arriving on that blistering sunny Sunday afternoon in mid-June, I found Chicago not to be that positive, overwhelming city that everyone had spoken so highly of; my eagerness was crushed. As I found Chicago a frightening city full of surprising and overpowering occurrences of uncertainties. To start with, inside an hour span of time, between our arrival at Chicago station and the drive to my brother Sim's apartment, I had seen the good, bad and ugly of some of Chicagoans' humanity. Even before we entered the terminal, I saw what seemed like thousands of people going to and from buildings that appeared to touch the sky!

Once inside the bus station, I saw the same kind of crowd going to and from the terminals; to leaving or looking for a loved one or cabs to take them to their destinations. After I had retrieved my luggage, found Sim and was in his car, I watched in anxiety as he attempted to exit the parking lot. I saw firsthand the stages of humanity in action. There were no considerations given to other drivers in their attempt to exit the parking lot. It was an outrageous display of bad temper and selfishness as Sim tried to carve his way into the flow of traffic, since no one wanted to give an inch. Once he was able to maneuver his way into the flow of traffic from the parking lot onto Madison Avenue. The drive to his apartment on the far Westside of Chicago seemed to take hours but was only about twenty minutes.

As Sim was maneuvering his way through what seemed to be another parking lot of traffic en route to his apartment, the music he was listening to on the radio was a bit more contemporary than what I was familiar with in Mississippi. The music selection in Mississippi in those days was Blues and some Top 40 Rock and Roll. Now that I understand the value of history, I find it fitting that the Blues originated in Mississippi, given our history, and then later was made famous in Chicago by Chess Records in 1947, the year I was born. I was honored to share my birth state with legendary blues artists from Mississippi like Muddy Waters, Howlin' Wolf, BB King, and songwriter Willie Dixon.

However, on that hot, sun-drenched Sunday afternoon, the Young Rascal's hits "Good Loving" and "Groovin' On A Sunday Afternoon" were the number-one songs being played on Chicago radio stations as Sim drove us to his apartment. The drive was filled with great adventures and somewhat intriguing. Seeing firsthand how many Chicagoans reacted to an in-progress incident of a crisis was an education in itself. I saw an elderly gentleman slumped over the steering wheel of his car as it veered to the right of us and plowed into a department store showcase on Madison Avenue. His foot must have been still on the accelerator after he crashed his car into a showcase window. The car engine was whining loudly as the left rear wheel spun, propelling smoke from it. As we drove by, I wondered what had caused that elderly gentleman to crash and where everyone was going in such a hurry that only two or three had stopped to help. Or if I was among that same moving crowd of passersby and had their agenda, what would I have done to assist him? As that unfortunate incident continued to unfold right in front of us, I saw humanity, for the most part, at its worst. Drivers on the same side of the street as the accident were blowing their horns frantically to maintain a continuous flow of traffic with little or no concern regarding the condition of the driver or the safety of those who were trying to help him. What an intense situation that was.

The Next Eye Opening Adventure...

It would take place within twenty-six blocks of that accident and Chicago's downtown miracle mile of Michigan Avenue and all its magnificent department stores. We were now traveling through the heart of Chicago's ghettos on the corner of Madison Avenue and California Street. What I was seeing for the first time were people who seemed to have been stripped of all their dignity. It was heartbreaking and an unbelievable sight to witness this devastating display of transgression and deceitfulness. I would later learn that a large percentage of that segregated society's occupants were uneducated and receiving some kind of general assistance. Neighborhood after neighborhood was feeding off each other's misery, which was and still is orchestrated by a systematic lifestyle that held them captive by a poor education system. Just like back in Mississippi. I saw con artists, prostitutes and drug sales, which caused entire communities to conform to lost dreams of hopefulness. This enslavement to evil and craftiness was mind-boggling to see and accept after so many had fought so hard to escape or rid themselves of similar evils in the Deep South. Little did I know, at that time, that one day I, too, would have no other choice but to dwell in a low-income, standardized living and become a part of one of those communities that was bordered by ghettos.

Lessons Learned

Oh, what an outstanding lesson God taught me that summer! I had to learn that I wasn't there to judge or understand why people willingly chose to live in the ghettos and never venture out no matter what circumstances may have been. Instead of judging them, I needed to pray for them and those who helped and hope that they found education as the way out. Also, I needed to remember Christ's parable He spoke concerning the poor: *"The poor you will always have with you, but you will not always have Me," (Mt 26:11)*. What an awesome free gift He has given those who believe. And as a believer, I shouldn't let the circumstances behind being poor be viewed as unbelief. My unbelief would only cultivate and feed opportunities for doubts to grow, leaving me vulnerable to being deceived, too. Not during this visit to Chicago but later in Oakland, I let those uncertainties in life take hold of my spirit. It only led me straight to sin and the misgivings that accompany it, and it all came with a very costly price tag. Those price tags belonged to an evil yet magical piper, Satan, who orchestrates this world system's sinful ways that compounded my life with a chemical addiction for the main purpose of driving my spirit and soul into a continuously delusional nightmare of lost HOPE. I called it, as many others did, having fun or doing "my thing," leaving God out of the picture. I was living a life of false hope whose end harvest was a lost soul. As a lost soul, I was depriving myself of God's free gift, His' precious promise of GRACE that says, *"Ask, and it will be given to you;* **Seek,** *and you will find;* **Knock,** *and it will be open to you," (Mt 7:7),* a promised land filled with everything your righteous heart desires is available for you, if you kept His' commandments.

Since I chose a sinful way of life after high school graduation, I was propelled into a lifestyle that did demand both my spirit and my soul for more than two decades. I will explain to you my sinful ways, the misgivings that accompany them, how they took me on a dangerous detour in life that was filled with false *hope* and promises. As I reflected back on those so called "good old days," I often wonder why God still loves me after I let evil's influences lead me away from Him. The way in which I let this piper's magic lead me away from God's truth and into a sinful life, which could have ended in a deadly tragedy for me. I was reminded of another magic piper from one of my favorite childhood fairy tales that did end in a tragedy for its town people.

My favorite fairy tale has been told in many different versions. The version I like the most can easily be applied to how I fell captive to the spell of a magic piper that possibly could parallel that of the people of Hamelin, who required the service of a piper to rid them of some rats from their city. Therefore, the moral of these two stories shouldn't come as a surprise. Everything in life comes with a price tag. So the lesson I learned was, I needed to consider which lifestyle I wanted to pay for and its effects. When I chose a sinful way of life, the cost was a broken spirit with all HOPE lost. When I returned to a life of righteousness, I was now eligible to receive that free gift, God's *grace*. Therefore, I had to remember that we are all God's children. Whether you were born into the wealth of old money that could have stemmed from some type of servitude or you were born into poverty, as I was, we are still God's children.

Yes! Believe it or not, we are all God's creations, His children. And we have been given a free will to choose our pathway in life, and a guide book, the Holy Bible, which outlines the consequences of good and evil. Even though God disciplines those who sin and blesses those who are righteous, He still loves all of us unconditionally, as is exemplified in Matthew 5:43-44: *"You have heard that it was said, 'You shall love your neighbor and hate your enemy'. But I say to you, love your enemies, bless those who curse you, do good to those who hate you, and pray for those who spitefully use you and persecute you."* Also in verse 45, *"that you may be sons of your Father in heaven; for He makes His sun rise on the evil and on the good, and sends rain on the just and the unjust."* It is here that we learn to walk and grow with God or grow stubbornly in our bitterness and take up revengeful ways.

I had to learn that there is a dimension of God's love that can only be experienced through forgiveness. I knew how important forgiveness was in life in order to receive God's blessing at an early age. And I had employed that forgivingness on many occasions growing up in Mississippi so I could be forgiven. Forgiving those con artists and drug dealers really tested my ability to its core for the first time. Especially after I saw a few of my relatives spending their hard-earned money from their labor-intensive jobs to buy subpar goods and materials in order to have extra money to spend on drugs and partying. How ironic that the jobs they worked the drug dealers turned down and thought were beneath them, but the money that was earned from these jobs was what kept them in business. For me, it resonated worse than the plantation owners who conned my relatives into working on "the half;" but they never received half, only low wages that always left them and Mom in debt, and she was never able to break even, let alone make a profit. Just like my relatives in Chicago, no matter how hard they worked, those parasites took every cent and they would never profit.

I had survived life's poverty and social injustice in the Deep South and heard of it in Chicago's ghettos. The talk of them had not done them justice. They were the most appalling, polluted and repulsive ways of living I had ever seen. Initially, I could not understand why anyone, especially my family, would want to live in an environment or communities such as those. How could the ghetto way of life continuously reach out and captivate *anyone*? Drugs, sex and anything you thought your heart desired was being sold on every one of the Chicago ghetto street corners and some of its surrounding communities. I saw young girls and ladies prostituting themselves for the price of a heroin or cocaine fix. My brother and others said that pimps habitually used everything from sophisticated methods of fear, intimidations or false positive influences of love, and being a father figure, to drugs in order to control their money-making establishment that earned some of them millions of dollars annually. Their enslaved female devotees were everywhere, flashing body parts, making lewd, salacious and suggestive innuendos to get your attention.

Sim turned to me and said, "I just wanted you to see this, and you are not to ever return to this part of Chicago," as we passed through without stopping!

The remainder of that summer

I did not go back into that part of Chicago other than as a passerby. Most of my time was spent working in a hot steel mill and trying to earn and save some money to purchase clothes and school supplies for the upcoming school year. Some would say that my initial visit to Chicago lacked excitement and fun, but that is definitely not so. Even with the hard, backbreaking work of that steel mill, I still had a great educational experience that summer. I was tempted numerous times by other party-going relatives and their friends to venture back into that part of Chicago, but I followed my brother's advice and stayed away. Instead, I spent my weekends looking for the safest parks or playgrounds possible where I could go and work on improving my basketball and baseball skills. Even though I didn't get many opportunities to participate in pickup baseball games, I did attend several and got a chance to watch some of Mississippi and Chicago's finest non-professional weekend legends perform. My brother Sim and Uncle JD's brothers-in-law,

John and Luther, had put together a baseball team that consisted of mostly former high school and recreational players from Mississippi. They played most often on Sunday in different parks on the south and west sides of Chicago. Often, I would attend those games to see them in action or hope for that opportunity to play myself if they needed a sub.

Then there were the former high school and college basketball aspiring NBA "stars" that I could pick up some moves from just by watching them play at different parks and playgrounds around the neighborhood. I had a great time watching, but it was even better when I got a chance to play. So as each week passed and the closer it got to the time I was to return home to prepare for my upcoming junior year in high school, the more things seemed to change for the better for me. I was making friends and had begun to learn my way around not only the Westside of Chicago but its south side. My brother Sim had started to trust me to drive his car, a 1965 Plymouth Fury. And I had started to really think about foregoing my junior year to stay in Chicago. Life seemed to be good with all my new friends, and I had a job that paid good money for my hard labor, much more then I could ever earn in Mississippi. So I began to really marvel just what life would be like for me if I stayed. However, a family member in-law made sure that didn't happen. This was the first time I recalled being conned into something so devious; this person told me it was okay for me to sleep in a bed that turned out to be "totally" off limits. This person also knew that as a steel mill worker my body would have absorbed the odor, dirt and grime of that place, and no matter how much or how often you took a bath or shower, its stench and filth stayed with you and would soil whatever you slept on.

So by being tricked into sleeping in that forbidden bed I was left without a place to stay for the remainder of that summer. I believe this happened because I was interfering with this person's ability to be involved in promiscuous activities. The fallout of this incident caused me to be quickly ushered out of Chicago and back to Mississippi, a blessing. I never spoke of that incident until this writing, and at the time I couldn't understand why that person wanted to get me in trouble and out of Chicago. Now I know that that incident happened for a reason and that God wanted me to return to Mississippi and finish high school. Chicago wasn't the place for me to be at that time in my life. Was I too gullible for Chicago, or did God have a job for me to finish in Mississippi?

Fortunately, three or four weeks prior to that deceitful incident, I learned that a special friend from Mississippi was spending her summer with her aunt and uncle on the far south side of Chicago in an affluent black neighborhood. The beauty of the situation was that her parents saw her as being above my social class in Mississippi but in Chicago they didn't have a voice. She would be leaving early to return to Mississippi not knowing that I would too be returning home sooner than planned. I wanted to spend as much time with her as possible before she and I had to leave for home. I was able to contact her. Her aunt and uncle were really nice people, even nice enough to invite me over for visits and before she had to return home for school I was able to take her to a movie in downtown Chicago. We had an enjoyable time at the movie and just taking in the sights of downtown Chicago.

Seeing Chicago at night for the first time with all its glittering lights, upscale movie theaters, restaurants, night clubs and department stores, even from the exterior, was a treat in itself. I began to understand why there were so many people going to and from the downtown area constantly every day and late into the night. Many of those individuals seemed to be tourists like us, trying to take in all of Chicago's magnificent sights in a short period of time. Chicago's downtown night scenery was so breathtaking that it could captivate a person into believing that it had everything a person needed and much more besides. As my summer vacation approached its screeching halt and the reality of returning to Mississippi began to set in, anger and annoyance began to flood my soul and spirit. But calmness won out because of the educational, life and spiritual experiences I had there! Fortunately, I also still had Wilma waiting for me back in Louise.

Back home

Things returned to the way they had been, separation by social classes of the have and have not. Everything from that summer was now a past memory of the good times as well as the bad times. Even though that was the last time my special friend and I were together socially, I never forgot her natural kindness and the loving friend she must have been to risk the repercussions from her family and friends back in Mississippi. If they had learned or had known about our short summer friendship, she would have faced some hardships.

Chapter 11

MY JUNIOR YEAR 1966-67 ...

II Corinthians 4:17: "For our light affliction, which is but for a moment, is working for us a far more exceeding and eternal weight of glory."

Funny how you can remember some things while totally shutting out others. For me, it was easy to remember the things that were pleasant and not the hurtful ones. As I look back on my junior year in high school, it started off with a bang; everyone seemed to be getting along well and becoming friends, or at least not enemies. Our football team had begun to show some promise by winning more games than we had lost the previous five seasons.

However, the most pleasant and dearest memories are those of Mom and Grandma and the things they taught me and the few minor disciplines. Other memories were of some people showing me loving kindness that lifted my spirit for who I was and not because I was an outstanding athlete or some popular person. Life had revealed to me that even if I have many great experiences, especially in sports, that one bad one can conquer all the good ones. For instance, our team consisted of Frank Washington, our five feet six inch guard; Ort James, our five feet five inch guard; Robert Cummings, our six feet six inch forward; Walter "Skip" Nutall, our six feet six inch power forward; and me, Joseph "Skeeter" Johnson, six feet four inch center. And a supporting cast of Clinton Chin, the best sixth man in the conference, along with other reserves: Cordell Mims and Andrew "Schultz" Williams helped us to win over ninety percent of our basketball games. Things were looking good for us to go to the state tournament that season in Jackson, Mississippi. All of our success could be contributed to two common goals: acceptance of the transfer athletic to build team spirit and teamwork with our objectives to win the Delta Conference Championship and go to the state tournament. After winning the Delta Conference Championship and being the smallest school ever to win it, our popularity and status in the tournament made us the giant slayer, "David." We were one game away from the state tournament and had to play Bolivar County High School at their venue. Our entire season would finally come down to one play by me that could put an end to our Cinderella season or put our school in the history book as being the smallest school from our conference to ever make it to the state tournament.

Cinderella's next stop

Our Cinderella journey takes us to Bolivar to play their home team. Would this be the place that David would finally be dethroned and our Cinderella run for the state tournament end or would we prevail and make history? As we were in the locker room getting dressed and Coach Woolfolk delivered his final game plan, there was an unpleasant feeling that came over me. One that couldn't be explained except there was a stillness about it that felt like it would never end; it would last forever. Once on the court and when our warm-up drills were over and the game finally started. It was like entering an eternity in motion, with only three or four points separating the teams the entire game. What a battle of wills that pushed and tested our limits for thirty-one minutes and fifty-five seconds in an atmosphere of sheer adrenaline and determination. I had never experienced anything like this before, and I didn't want it to end. Over that duration in time, not only could I feel my own pains and joys as the game took us on a rollercoaster ride for those thirty-one minutes and fifty-five seconds, I felt our fans' and especially coach Woolfolk's pains and joys, too. It all came down to free throws to decide which team would advance to the state tournament in Jackson, Mississippi. Those two free throws were awarded from a dreaded turnover by my hands! The same hands just a week ago played a significant role in winning the Delta Conference Championship. How quickly things can change in life. I had now given the ball to my opponent with only five seconds remaining on the game clock, and we were down by one point. Once the ball was made ready for play and inbounded, we were left with no other choice but to foul immediately, and Ore did. The foul put their best player at the free throw line for one and one free throws, if made, could ice the game for them! As we were lining up for the free throws, I began to pray, asking God not to let him make those free throws so I would have a chance to redeem my mistake.

As he stepped up to the free throw line, a distressing feeling came over me as my heart was beating rapidly. As he released that first free throw, a sheer stillness employed my body so that I could not even remember what the atmosphere of what the crowd was like. As I continued to pray from him to miss and possibly there were many others praying to God, as well: Those who wanted us to win, and those who wanted them to win; so whose prayers would God answer? As if God was playing a role in that basketball game! The first free throw attempt hit nothing but the bottom of the net, putting them up by two points. It's funny that I can't remember the precise score but everything that led up to it and after it. It seems that the whole assemblage took a deep breath and held it as did he for that next free throw attempt. The silence was broken as his next free throw did not penetrate the net as did first one. A timeout...giving them a two point advance with now five seconds left in the game. Coach set up our play for that last-second shot, hoping for a deadlock, which I practiced many times but had never before had to use until that game. The play coach drew up called for a series of off-ball screens to free up Ort or Frank as first options for that last-second desperation shot. I was to be the inbounder of the ball and the second option. As the play unfolded, Ort became open and I made the pass to him for that final shot. As he launched a half-court shot toward the goal and it seemed to take minutes for it to reach the goal, as those seconds had expired. There was an eruption of cheers from their fans as Ort's shot bounced off the front of the rim to the court giving them the win. Our fans stared in shock as their players and fans celebrated the victory. What a heart-breaking loss that was to take. I and a few teammates fell to the court in disbelief, watching their jubilation.

To this day, I still blame myself for losing that game even after I learned a year later of the corruption that possibly played a major role in the outcome of that game and others. How money was being wagered, that a certain player on OUR team would score twenty points or more in each of our games. This made things much clearer to me why he took the majority of the shots, even if they were bad shots. For him, the game that I had grown to love for its team spirit and play was not about team at all or those common goals and objectives; it was all about self-accomplishment and money at the cost of his team-mates' hard work and efforts to win that elusive prize, a state championship. Learning that a teammate of mine, and being from such a small school as Montgomery High School (300+) had corruptions tied to it, was more devastating than losing the final game. I had worked so hard at improving my game and waited for a year to be a starter and another year to get a chance at winning it all. But loss and dishonesty had played a major role in it, and it was sickening for me. For the longest time, I thought that all my transgressions were related to losing that game and the corruption that surrounded it. However, I knew that I must take full responsibility for my wrongdoing and not blame others or how I tried to blame God for not bailing me out of that dreaded turnover causing that heart breaking defeat for us and a jubilating win for them.

1 Corinthians 15: 33-34: Do not be deceived; evil company corrupts good habits–Awake to righteousness, and do not sin, for some do not have the knowledge of God. Paul, speak this to your shame.

Over the next two decades or so, gradually I began to spin out of control and to hang out with the wrong crowd. I had involved myself in things I once felt to be reprehensive for anyone to defile themselves that way. As the years passed, I continued to believe that God would take care of me no matter what I did as long as I didn't hurt anyone else. Not realizing that my integrity was being eaten away by my iniquity. Deep down inside I knew that God wasn't the cause of this certain change in my integrity or for the loss of that game. I just was looking for someone or something other than myself to blame!

My junior year ended somewhat like the end of that basketball season, with uncertainty, and Mom finally getting tired of the treatment she was receiving from her last husband. He had already run his oldest son and daughter and my sister away. There was also continuous fighting between him and his second oldest son. I continued to stay away from the house as much as possible and did what I was told to keep problems away from Mom. She had enough to deal with without me adding to her troubles by being defiant when it came to my responsibilities around the house. Even if I had to do things that weren't my responsibility, I still did them if she asked me to. I could sense that things were not going as well as they did when we first moved to Louise and Mom had started to experience some of the problems that her husband's first wife had experienced with him. She was growing tired of his infidelity and lying about money, as well as his aggressive nature to control the house. With his older children and my sister Lueretha gone, his anger began to be directed toward Mom. So! Finally! One day, Mom came to me with this faraway look in her eyes and said, "I have made arrangements for you, Jessie and James [my two younger brothers], and myself to move to Chicago." She asked if I wanted to go with her or move back to Anchor Curve to live with my Aunt Pearle and Uncle Joe Willie to finish my last year of school. I chose to move back to Anchor Curve. Mom had saved up some money and purchased tickets for us to take the Greyhound bus to Chicago. But since she only had to purchase three tickets instead of four with me staying in Mississippi meant she had some extra money for the trip, which was good. Now I was back at Anchor Curve living with Aunt Pearle and Uncle Joe Willie for approximately three or four weeks before the opportunity came for Mom and my two younger brothers to leave for Chicago. One hot summer week day, when her husband left for the day to work the fields Mom, Jessie and James, with just the clothes on their backs, took the Greyhound bus to Chicago to never return to him or Louise.

The cotton field era ends

Finally, the cycle was broken and Mom, generations later, was out of those horrible cotton fields; under no circumstance did I want her and my two younger brothers to ever return, not even for my high school graduation. Yet knowing exactly what kind of lifestyle they had to look forward to, since I had lived the previous summer on Chicago's Westside, and just what they had in store for them, I still wanted them out of Mississippi from all the turmoil we had to face each day. However, that happiness I wanted for Mom and my two brothers would be short-lived. Now due to her lack of education and lack of industrial working skills, Mom was forced into the ranks of unemployment that led to welfare assistance. They learned what I had learned that prior summer; what the words poor and ghetto really meant, for they were in the middle of it!

Living on the Westside of Chicago was as different from living in Mississippi as dawn is to dusk. Chicago terrified Mom, Jessie and James. For instance, James and Jessie were chased to and from school daily by delinquents who wanted them to join their street gang. This act of recruitment eventually led my two younger brothers to refuse to attend school out of fear and became house poor, uneducated refugees. From my perspective, this was just another way our government and educational systems failed and denied urban children their freedom to an education. Many street gang members are the direct result of decades of uneducated people that came from slavery and sharecroppers and migrated to the northern states and didn't receive proper training skills to become self-sufficient. Instead, they were allowed to become dependent on a system to take care of them, and eventually that system became the authority in their home instead of the parents. This same system took away my Mom's ability to discipline my younger brothers and imposed their rules within her home in order for her to receive subsidy benefits from a system to survive, as did thousands before and after her. Being a welfare recipient was similar to sharecropping when it came to making a living; both were subsidy institutions. As a sharecropper, she had to work additional hours at the Big Boss Man's house to earn that extra needed money. In Chicago, she had to work in Kathryn's Soul Food restaurant's sizzling hot kitchen as a cook to earn that required extra money that paid less than minimum wages. This was heart-breaking for me.

I imagine for them this was more terrifying than working the cotton fields while fighting off snakes that sought the cool shelter underneath the cotton vegetation. Mom, Jessie and James were now literally fighting for their lives. Like all the others who had been enslaved into the injustices of what Chicago's ghettos had to offer them in her insidious but somewhat subtle way of continuing to hide her true existence. However, it's not always what we want to happen in life that will actually happen. From my experience, it is our human nature to think that God will not do what His word says, especially in our time of trouble when things in our life seem to be going backward instead of forward. This is the time when we should really trust Him. Our trials and tribulations only intensify when our blessing is on the horizon, trying to detour our faith in God's words. Each time when I was about to receive a blessing from God, it seemed like my whole world would come crashing down on me.

Education came hard for me. With my junior year coming to its end and my senior year waiting for me, I still had not accepted nor wanted to allow God to outline my future without sports at the forefront. All the punishments and ridicules I had to suffer at the hands of teachers and peers from elementary through junior high was only another attempt to keep me from finishing high school and remaining uneducated. That way I wouldn't be able to do what God had planned out for my life. However, I continued to strive for the wrong crown...the wrong pinnacle!

Chapter 12

FINALLY

*Deuteronomy 3:22: "You must not fear them, for
the Lord your God Himself fights for you"*

My senior year 1967-68, I was living back at Anchor
Curve. I didn't have much time for anything
except school and sports. With Montgomery High School
located on the south end of Louise, four miles northwest
of Anchor Curve, each evening's extracurricular activities, e.g., sock hops, basketball games, football games or
homecoming, my first priority was to secure that first ride
home. Usually that was Coach Woolfolk, who lived in
Yazoo City, or my friend Robert Davis, who lived a few
miles below me.

Therefore, as much as I wanted to hang out with my
girlfriend and some of the other guys and girls after our
basketball games or occasionally enjoy some of the good
times at other extracurricular activities, I couldn't. To
hang around for any of those evening activities without
that guaranteed ride home would have been detrimental to

149

my health, if not a death sentence. For me at that time in my life, no pleasures, good or bad, were worth risking my life. Some taunted me as a coward and chickenhearted, but as I look back on those trying times, they dictated what one's safety required. I say that I was letting God's wisdom lead me. On the few times that I didn't have a ride, I would hide in the tall grass alongside the highway until cars passed. This was a normal occurrence on our community roads.

No ride home placed me in a dangerous situation similar to the danger of speaking against the sharecropping régime. If you had looked a white man in the eyes and told him what you thought, even if it was not offensive, and God forbid if you didn't walk around like ostriches with your head lowered to the ground and inadvertently made eye contact with a white female, there would have been serious consequences. Your ass was grass and they were the lawn mower! We just wanted to be respected and treated like human beings. I had exceeded the usual age of seventeen when many black males were sent to live with relatives in the northern cities of Chicago or Detroit. I had to be very careful about what I said or did or places I went because even the thought of standing up for oneself was seen as being disrespectful or defiant in the eyes of many white males, and this kind of behavioral display would and did lead to serious repercussions and even death. If there was suspicion of any kind that you were even contemplating such ideas or ideas of rebellion, there would be a serious price to pay. The KKK had a reputation of inflicting deadly harm upon those who bucked or questioned their master's or plantation owner's system of power and control.

The plantation owners' and many other white men's superiority had become more prevalent to me my senior year. Now it was my turn to become that threat to them and their ways of dominating my family, just like my older brothers, uncles and cousins had become that threat. I was no longer that boy who carried water, worked in their home with Mom and cared for their cosmetic lawns. This change of command had now filled me with great concern for my safety, and I needed to make sure that my grades were good enough to graduate so I would be able to leave Mississippi alive! I know it is hard for some people to believe this type of brutality happened just over 40 years ago, and it might sound dramatic but it was very real. I lived it every day! Nothing mattered for me accept fulfilling my academic requirements to rid myself of this stigma of being a failure and nothing more than another uneducated sharecropper. I could not succumb to a way of life of being treated less than what my Creator had created me to be, a Human Being, in His own image, who says that I can do all things through Him who strengthens me, *Philippians 4:13*! Therefore, I was left with no choice but to devote all my time and energy to my academics that would ultimately secure my graduation from high school. My commitment to academics demanded so much of my time, it placed a handicap on extracurricular activities. My friends and fellow athletes questioned my manhood and commitment to the game of basketball, which I once so dearly loved. My learning disabilities at the time seemed like a death sentence or a curse had been placed on me. In order to cope, I had to rid myself of everything that interfered with my academic life if I was to graduate, do I dare say, on time!

Eliminating distractions

One of the hardest things I had to do in my life was to turn all of my attention away from sports and focus on academics, especially since I had become such a popular figure around school and in our community. Not to mention that one loss by my hands had stopped me and my teammates from the state tournament in Jackson, Mississippi. Every high school athlete's dream is to go to a state tournament in their individual sport. I had to realize that even if we did make it to the state tournament my senior year, it wouldn't aide me one bit in graduating from high school. I would be stuck working in those cotton and soybean fields my entire life. It would be the same fate as those who let sports come before academics and only attend school for the sole purposes of athletics, and when their individual sport season ended, so did their enthusiasm for school. I wasn't about to become one of those sports enthusiasts who stayed in school into their early and mid-twenties just to play sports. I wanted to graduate high school and move on in life outside of Mississippi. I did not even let my newly found popularity, which was a sure way to indulgence in transgressions, interfere with my need to improve academically. I eliminated any and all things that would cause me to fall short of having the required credits needed to graduate; as you may recall, I was already older than my classmates. I had to enhance my opportunities to go to college and succeed in life. If I had not placed academics first, I wouldn't have known how to apply it in college.

Graduation ceremony

The night of my graduation was filled with mixed emotions of joy, dismay and surprise. I was extremely happy; you can even say that I was overjoyed to be done with high school. I was also saddened to be leaving my girlfriend, Ora Lee "Gold," and other friends. I was shocked to learn I was being recognized for something other than my athletic abilities by being honored with a Citizenship Award. At the time I did not understand why or who would vote for me to receive such a prestigious award. And for what reason or reasons was I being recognized with this important honor? Could it be some kind of cover up for my corporal punishment days of humiliation in elementary and junior high school; or was it for how I openly accepted the students from Midnight and Silver City and risked losing my own friends?

Through the remainder of the ceremony I went over and over it in my mind, what was the true meaning behind this recognition? It was my understanding that the Citizenship Award was to recognize those students who worked hard at being good citizens at home, at school and in the community. I was never officially informed as to why I was being recognized. After the conclusion of the ceremony, and once we, the graduates, had marched outside and began intermingling with our social groups, I let out a roar of relief and astonishment that could be heard all over the school grounds, saying, "Yes, I am done. Thank God almighty I am done." I never did find out who nominated me and why I received this award, but I was surprised to get it and enjoyed the moment.

153

Fortuitously, when my daughter and son were in middle school, they both received the same award!

But the joy was short-lived because I had not received any offers to attend any local junior colleges, let alone a four-year college or university. What was I to do? BECOME A FARMER hahaha, and remain in Mississippi for the rest of my life as predicted by some of my teachers. The last thing I wanted to happen in my life was to make them right! Especially after I had given up so much to make sure I had enough academic credits to graduate.

Once again I was in the wait-and-see mode. I was waiting to hear from Coach Woolfolk to see if any local junior colleges, colleges or universities were interested in me. I had no letters of intent from any colleges as there were for other students, such as the kids from the affluent families who had better grades than me. Trying to figure it all out by myself really began to make me doubt that I would ever be able to attend any college or university. Even if accepted, how would I earn enough money for college if I did not receive some kind of scholarship or aid? There were no school counselors to help me with these dilemmas.

What was I to do? Stay and work in Anchor Curve and be just another sharecropper, or return to Chicago to be with Mom and my two younger brothers in the ghetto? I couldn't even purchase a ticket if I wanted to. Before I realized it, it was mid-June, one of those hot, steamy summer days; I was sitting outside in the shade of my uncle and aunt's front porch, trying to keep cool and mulling over my future. I saw Mr. Lawrence Macklin, the plantation owner, driving down the highway towards our house in his truck. I thought he was on his way to check on my uncle and his other workers or going to his office at my best friend Al's house. (I know it seems odd that Mr. Macklin's office was in my friend's house, but it was; he owned the land and the house, so he used it how he pleased.) But when he pulled into the driveway of my uncle and aunt's house, I started to wonder if something was wrong with Uncle Joe Willie. As he drove into the yard, he had this look on his face as if he had come to fulfill the prophecy of my teachers. As he walked closer, I could tell that he wasn't coming because something was wrong or to have a general conversation. He had come to speak with me for some reason, and I began to wonder why.

Maybe my Uncle Joe Willie had told him that I would be staying with them until college started in the fall and he wanted me to work for him. If so, that would be great. I could make some money while waiting to hear from Coach about college. After an exchange of pleasantries, he asked me if I wanted to work for him the remainder of the summer. He knew that education emancipation was causing him a problem since sharecroppers' children were now being educated and going off to colleges and not becoming field hands. So who was going to be there to work his fields?

I agreed to work for him and began to wonder just what kind of job he had in mind for me. He asked if I would drive one of his tractors to do cultivation, I agreed. He asked me when I could start, and I replied: "Tomorrow," and he begun to walk toward his truck without telling me what his pay rate was going to be. As he walked away, I asked about the hourly pay rate. He said thirty cents per hour.

Without hesitation I asked him if he thought that "I was a damn fool to drive his tractor for thirty cents an hour when the nation's minimum wage was $1.40 an hour!" I knew this from working in the steel mill of Chicago that previous summer. His face turned beet red as he immediately turned and walked back to his truck without saying a word, got in it and quickly drove off. Immediately, I knew that there would be hell to pay for that comment to him, so I returned to what I was doing; trying to figure out ways to speed up getting in a college or a university with my time now literally running out on my stay in Mississippi!

So that evening, when my uncle came home from driving tractor, he asked me what I said to Mr. Lawrence (we called him by his first name but of course had to add Mr.) because he had asked my uncle what was wrong with me! So I explained to my uncle and aunt just what transpired between us. They must have called Mom and Coach (to see if he had heard from a school) because after a couple of days I was ushered out of Anchor Curve en route to Oakland, California, where my three older brothers and a cousin were living. This was done for my safety.

Chapter 13

OAKLAND, CALIFORNIA...

Matthew 4:1: "Jesus was led by the Spirit into the wilderness to be tempted of the devil."

I thought the summer of 1966 in Chicago had prepared me for anything. But I was wrong. And the following events will show how I let myself fall prey to an immoral lifestyle that consisted of self-gratification in Satan's wilderness of sins. Which led me to believe that I wasn't doing anything wrong because it was according to man's status and laws, not God's.

Oakland! Midsummer 1967 was a city that offered many opportunistic, immoral, captivating lifestyles that were waiting for me at many street corners to drag me or you into its whirlwind of deceitfulness! I got caught up in that whirlwind of dangerous drugs that were accompanied by many sexual opportunities. It seized me into an addictive way of life that no person should have to encounter. Especially a young man just out of high school, regardless if he was from the blighted cotton fields of Mississippi like me or any small towns in America; he shouldn't be allowed to roam her streets unsupervised. I know from experience, although initially I found Oakland not to be as frightening and full of surprises as was Chicago. What was overpowering was the Greyhound bus ride through six states with stops in roughly twenty-nine cities over a span of approximately forty-eight hours.

This awesome adventure started as the Greyhound bus exited the terminal in Memphis, Tennessee. I started to wonder if this trip had anything in store for me as fascinating or intriguing as Chicago's magnificent miracle mile of Michigan Avenue and all its elegance. In my awakened state of mind, I wondered if I would see firsthand some of God's magnificent, amazing and frightening creations that others had often spoken of as I boarded that greyhound bus.

Once onboard and as we were about to enter the state of Arkansas, I thought maybe not; because thus far I haven't seen anything that could measure up to Chicago. But shortly thereafter, out of nowhere appeared miles of Arkansas' magnificent pines, the state's official tree, which seemed to touch the sky. From my window seat, I had to lean downward to see the tops of those pine trees as the bus traveled through them. It seemed like it took hours to get through them, but it was much less than that, of course; more like minutes. The thrill of seeing those superb Arkansas pines had given this sharecropper's son something to remember for life, and I even contemplated returning one day to see them again. I also thought if these few pines around Little Rock looked so magnificent, just how gorgeous the ones would be around Pine Bluff!

The thrill of seeing those towering pines trees was swept away from my sight as soon as they appeared. The next fifteen or twenty hours took us through urban and rural cities like Oklahoma City and El Reno, Oklahoma, and into Amarillo, Texas, without much scenery, as the first day came to an end. But that was on the outside; on the inside there were two beautiful sisters that boarded the bus in Little Rock en route to Oakland as I was! We were the only young adults on the bus, and it didn't take long before we engaged in conversation. The youngest sister of the two, who looked to be about my age, initiated the conversation with me, asking "was this my first time visiting the West Coast?" After talking across the aisle for a few minutes, Sheila, the younger sister, asked if she could sit with me and I said yes! Into and throughout that night we talked about each other's likes and dislikes and to remain friends once in Oakland. From her conversation, I could tell that Sheila and her sister had made this trip before, and Sheila was more advanced in the FACTS OF LIFE (the birds and the bees) and city life than I was. As we traveled through the rest of Texas, only stopping for a ten or fifteen-minute rest period to get something to eat or to stretch our legs, I learned more about male and female intimacy from her than I had learned in my whole life up to that point. I did not let her know that she was giving me the education I had been looking. Naturally, most of my learning was from verbal communication, with some late night cuddling and kissing, since we were on a bus!

The next morning, I woke up to find her still holding on to my arm and to find we had traveled through the great Sonora and Mojave deserts and were now in the state of California near Los Angeles, our next scheduled rest stop. I was somewhat saddened and disappointed that I did not get the chance to see those great deserts. But I was glad to have been in the company of such a lovely and affectionate young woman for that long and tiresome trip. After a thirty-minute rest stop, we were leaving the city of Angels, LA, with three stops remaining before our arrival in Oakland.

My excitement grew as we exited the Greyhound bus station not so much to see the smog-covered LA or a movie star, but to finally get to Oakland and off that bus. My bad knees were killing me along with my back. I played the tough guy role and did not let on how bad my knees and back were really hurting. I did not want to leave a wimpy impression of me with my traveling companion, who I might never see again after our arrival in Oakland.

To my surprise, there was something waiting ahead of me that would test my courage more than my aching knees and back in front of Sheila. Within approximately an hour span of time after departing the Greyhound bus station in LA, en route to Bakersfield about ninety miles away, I had seen the good, bad and ugly of LA's humanity from afar and that was close enough for me. I had seen similar images of thousands of people going to and from buildings that didn't appear to touch the skies as they did in Chicago!

Once outside the city limits and far-off in the distance was another unbelievable stretch of highways. I saw some devastating mountains that did appear to touch the skies as their peaks disappeared into the clouds placing a greater fear over me, knowing that we had to travel through them in order to get to Oakland! This fear that they had placed over me was so great that if I had sufficient money and the choice, I would have taken the next bus back through the flat lands and deserts to home. But I had to be brave and not show any fear in the presence of my traveling friends. Then it came to me that this must be the stretch of historic highway that gets its name from the grapevines of California because of its twisting highway that outlined those magnificent but terrifying mountains that connect southern and northern California. I had heard my brothers and others talk of them when they came home to visit. They said this is one of most beautiful and most traveled pieces of highway in the United States, which would complete this long and tiresome trip. They said the Grapevine, old Highway 99, was built in stages starting in the 1950s and wouldn't be completed until the 1980s and would be renamed Interstate 5. This final stretch of a forty-hour-plus bus ride would last another four hours plus, and there was no way vehicle travelers could avoid the wrath of the Grapevine. This stretch of highway had overpowering heights of winding elevations, and its downward grade would be frightening, yet breath-taking, with each ascent and descent into its mountain range!

I gave thanks to God that our bus made it through without incident. The history of this stretch of highway dictates that it's not just older cars that don't make it through the Grapevine. If any motorists ignore the warning signs, telling them to turn off their air conditioning as they ascend and descend into the mountains, then your car might be choked by the grapevine. It affected my eyes and my ears popped with each slow climb to its top and fast descent down to its bottom. One could give the analogy that you were in God's heavens and falling to hell gates, on earth, at least it felt that way to me!

My arrival

What a relief it was to finally arrive at the Oakland Alameda Greyhound bus station! I retrieved my luggage and exchanged pleasantries with Sheila's sister before Sheila and I exchanged phone and address information and but it was likely our final good-by. We actually saw each other one more time that summer, and then I never saw her again. As I exited the bus station with Willie, who made that brilliant catch while playing center field at Montgomery High School, for the drive to his home I was astonished to see that he owned a brand-new 1966 white Convertible Corvette! Another surprise as we exited the bus station parking lot, I saw firsthand the dissimilar laid-back style of Californian humanity in action, much different from that of the Chicagoan humanity, especially drivers. However, there were many other corrupt similarities between Chicago and Oakland and not just the ones that captured me, the drugs and make-love-not-war lifestyle, which nearly destroyed my life during my visit. The most devastating consequence for succumbing to this world system lifestyle has always been lost educational opportunities. I know this from personal experience. Those lost educational opportunities for me didn't allow me to be able to read and fully understand just what God wanted from me. I knew that God would forgive me of my sins if I asked in Jesus' name, and God has anointed preachers to preach His word and lead us out of bondage from transgression and sins; but then I couldn't tell you where to find it in the Bible.

Back in high school, God had showed me why it was so important to be educated. So I didn't have to totally depend on His anointed leaders to deliver His message to me only on Sundays. Being educated allows me to be feed on His word, to do His will each day if I choose to and not just on Sundays. Don't take this the wrong way. I knew that I needed His anointed ones, but I also needed to be able to read His word myself. But I let my fleshly desires of wanting to be accepted by my new social crowd, ignoring God's warnings. So guess what, the leader of this world system then and even now wants me as an uneducated human being to remain ignorant to the power that God's word has, for his sole purpose of controlling my life. I myself failed to realize and accept that there were only so many positions available in any sport, and it is impossible for everyone who tries out to get selected. But with an education and God on my side, who can be against you when it comes to the opportunities out there for anyone who is willing to work hard, trust and believe.

Psalm 75:6 & 7: "For exaltation comes neither from the east nor from the west nor from the south. But God is the Judge: He puts down one, and exalts another .But God is the Judge!" In other words, God is in control over who gets promoted and receives leadership positions.

The world teaches us that the way to get ahead is to claw your way to the top and to get it while you can; that's "Vanity!" Since we can't take them (material possessions, and all pleasure under the sun) with us and control what the benefactors do with them, how and what they will use them for, if not for the glory of God's kingdom, then that also is "Vanity." However, the Bible teaches us that the way to honor is through humility and service. This is not to say that we should not develop our talents and seek opportunities for growth and advancement; but in all things, we should put the LORD first! But just because I knew that an education was one of the most important things one needs in life to do God's work, it was another thing to conform to God's way of getting things done.

Just like when I had my first ride from the bus station in Chicago the songs that were being played over the radio; Gladys Knight & the Pips, The Temptations, Marvin Gaye and of course Aretha Franklin, weren't the typical music I was familiar with in Mississippi. The drive to Willie's home wasn't as intense as the one from Chicago's bus station to Sim's apartment. This gave me time to think of what I was going to do with my life and basketball. Though I quickly forgot about both.

Oakland did have something wonderful to offer, and for me it was the community that Willie lived in. I was only five blocks from the Oakland-Alameda County Coliseum–home to the Oakland Raiders and Oakland Athletics; also home to the Golden State Warriors. I could walk to the games and could hear and see the fireworks display from each home football and baseball games just as clear as if I were at the games in person. Life was good, but I was missing my friends back home, but not Mississippi itself. After a few months of illustrations and instructions from my brothers, I had learned my way around Oakland well enough to get to the important places I needed to go on my own: to my brothers Sim (who had moved to Oakland within 6 months of my last summer visit) and Sam's apartments; downtown Oakland; and the parks that held pickup games of basketball, bordered by East 14th Street and MacArthur Boulevard, Bancroft Ave, with 98th Street as my northern latitude guide. I was now on my own, learning my way around the city which claims to have some of the finest bars, clubs and restaurants, and I wanted to sample them all.

Summer of 1968

It had been several months since I was ushered out of Anchor Curve for refusing to work for Mr. Lawrence. Yet there I was allowing my spirit and integrity to be imprisoned as I had surrendered to the fads that we all associate with "make love not war," a whirlwind tour of the sexual revolution in America! Many in my generation smile when they think of this time in our history—and don't get me wrong; I had a lot fun, but the psychedelic haze took over! That fad's desires led me to the free-spirited young ladies of Oakland to fulfill my morally wrong behavior. I had now turned away from being that simple, God-fearing, sport-loving, enthusiastic young man from Mississippi and didn't know just how long this insatiable thirst would last. I was no longer naïve, yet I was still gullible. This lifestyle had removed my desire to play any sport, except for an occasional pickup game of basketball with my brother Willie and his friends at the neighborhood park. I had no aspirations for a daily workout routine to keep my game razor-sharp just in case Coach would call. Basketball at a college level was the furthest thing from my mind.

Willie, whom I lived with most of the time, tried to warn me, as well as Sam and Sim. The only thing I had to remind me of home was an occasional letter from my girlfriend Gold. Reading and writing had become my least favorite tools for communication, since it was so difficult for me to write complete sentences. Therefore, to stay in touch with her I would often call her. Of course, this ran up Willie's phone bill to several hundred dollars. He didn't seem to mind that much, but I realized that I had caused a huge financial setback that would be a problem between him and his wife. I did offer to pay the bill, but Willie being Willie would not have any of it. He just said to cut back on the calling or let her call me sometimes. I called less and wrote more short and simple sentences using her words to answer her questions. I was also surprised after being in Oakland for a while to find out that my friend Frank, fellow basketball player, was in town. We hung out a few times and later ended up leaving together to go back to Mississippi.

Willie had helped me get a good job shortly after my arrival working for a hand-crafted furniture store. This helped me to get off to what I thought would be bigger and better things. Although I was good at working with my hands, making furniture did not "cut" it for me due to my limited math skills. I was let go. Within weeks, I had another job for the uneducated, working for Del Monte Foods on the assembly line. I met this guy named Jack; soon we befriended each other. Shortly thereafter, I learned that Jack and I had something in common more than working on the assembly line. We both had a great compassion for and a serious crush on the same actress, Sophia Loren. Each chance I got, I went to see as many of her movies as possible. Jack said that she had a home in Oakland Hills and he knew where it was. And we both agreed that we should one day drive by hoping that we might catch a glimpse of her in person. But we were afraid to do so, because we did not know what people would think, if they saw a male salt and pepper team cruising around in their prosperous neighborhood, even if I drove my brother's Corvette. So we just admired her from afar in her movies! With all the mayhem that was taking place in Oakland during that time, with the Black Panthers organization that was at odds with the local police and the FBI over the Bobby Hutton shooting incident, we kept a low profile.

Not only did I have Willie's 1966 white Corvette, I also had Sam's 1962 red Mustang and Sim's 1965 silver Chevy SS Super Sport. So each day after work and on weekends, needless to say I had a choice of three great cars to cruise up and down East 14th Street, scoping out young ladies I thought would be impressed with anyone those cars. After weeks of cruising up and down East 14th Street, I was not making any progress towards my goal; like any other 20 year old, even though I had a girlfriend back home, I wanted to find that special girl or girls who would fill all my desires. To my surprise, I realized that there were young ladies from my brother's neighbors who were more than willing to fulfill my needs. So I started seeing a nineteen-year-old girl, Linda, who I didn't know had a boyfriend, and a supposed divorcee, Barbara, but I think her husband was actually an off-shore worker, to achieve my goals. I thought that as long as I did not play games with their feelings by not lying to them about my intentions, I wasn't doing anything wrong. Although this type of behavior was acceptable because of the fad of the sexual revolution, it was not normal for this young man from Mississippi with a strong Christian upbringing. My moral integrity had succumbed to my desires. Like the rest of my new social group, I thought I was immortal. I had become thoughtless in my desires to be with my two female companions and keep my girl back home.

I often wondered where it all was coming from and why I had continued to defile myself that way. Was it because of my learning disability or maybe my early cornfield episode, or was it from some kind of rejection I suppressed that caused me to put myself in harm's way? I would go clubbing in Jack London Square with my young lady friend or my divorcee and did not care who saw me there with either of them. One night in particular, I was in one of my preferred nightclubs with my young lover and there was her boyfriend and two of his friends. I thought for sure that this encounter with them was going to cause a serious problem. That was the first time I felt any fear of the lifestyle I was leading. As we sat at our table, they stared at us and when I wasn't looking they threw pieces of crushed ice at her. When I attempted to say something to them, she insisted that if I did that it would only make things worse, we should just leave.

As I was about to stand up one of them threw a piece of ice and hit me on the arm. Once I stood up, they immediately stopped and turned their attention away from our table. They must have been intimidated by my size and height because they didn't even make eye contact with me as I walked by them. But then I was hit in the back with what I thought was another piece of ice after I had proceeded past their table on our way out of the nightclub.

She apologized for their behavior and said he wasn't her boyfriend anymore and that I shouldn't worry about them doing anything to me. That incident did place some concern in my mind about how I had let my need control how I was living life.

In the meantime, the only other true fears or concerns I had while adventuring through those radical streets of Oakland was the Black Panthers organization. I had been told by my brothers, along with my first cousin William, "Honey" as we all called him, the son of my Aunt Pearl and Uncle Joe Willie, and my second cousin Derrick's father, to stay as far as possible away from anyone that was associated with that organization. So the safest places to hang out, at least compared to the Black Panthers, other than the clubs, were the house parties where you could get anything your heart desired. There was drugs, sex or just "chilling" and watching all the different personalities trying to find love in all the wrong places, just as I was. Isn't it funny how something totally out of character can end up initially being more gratifying than what you had intended it to be? After everything that I had done in my prolonged but relatively short stay in the City by the Bay, the most memorable turned out to be the Wax Museum at Fisherman's Wharf in San Francisco. Seeing the replicas that sculptors had recreated with such a likeness of their subjects in a wax image gave me such a fright. I was fascinated to learn that these sculptors armed only with photographs and actual measurements of their subjects, used lumps of wax to create a perfectly proportioned imagery of near-life resemblance that was unbelievable and creepy.

Does this remind you of another Sculptor as it did me, who created a replica of Himself from the dust of the Garden of Eden and breathed the breath of life into its nostrils? The very same One we ask to mold us as a potter molds their clay. My Sculptor knew that I needed a change from the City by the Bay. And the change came with a phone call from Aunt Pearl saying that Coach Woolfolk had made arrangements for me and Frank to attend Natchez Junior College in Natchez, Mississippi. In retrospect, it wasn't all about Natchez Junior College; it was about getting me out of Oakland to save me from myself, although my aunt didn't know that. I had become too comfortable working for Del Monte Foods on their assembly line and roaming the streets of Oakland for opportunities to become more involved with the fads that would be more prominently associated with the 70s. With reluctance, I left Oakland and thought that I had left behind an addicted lifestyle I had grown to love and headed home to Anchor Curve. Young and ignorant, I did not know that I had allowed myself to surrender to a lifestyle of sensuality that would haunt me for decades.

Chapter 14

COAHOMA JUNIOR COLLEGE VIA NATCHEZ JUNIOR COLLEGE

James 3:15: "This wisdom does not descend from above, but is earthly, sensual, demonic."

Natchez Junior College, what can I say about it! Except that as Frank and I approached its campus by taxicab that crisp, sunny Saturday afternoon in September 1969, I could see the college grounds off in the distance, outlining a steep hill looking more like an old Army barracks than a college campus. Once on campus and somewhat settled in our room I attempted to get accustomed to my new surroundings with a short tour of the other dormitories. The strangest feeling started to come over me, as if someone or something was watching me, and it went on throughout that night. This made me feel as though I had now been placed in some kind of mystical dimension. Or was my addiction to Oakland's nightlife and its amenities, i.e., drug culture, making me feel these strange feelings, the feeling that someone, or some spirit mostly likely (sensual or the Holy Spirit), was trying to speak to me? That next morning my dilemma was to figure out which one of my spirits was speaking to me, or perhaps it was Mom? Whichever one it was, I did not know what to make of it or why it was happening.

Was it something or was it someone who was watching over me; whatever one it was, it made me feel really uncomfortable. So it wasn't God, right, since He doesn't operate that way. The following Monday morning, an episode between two professors during orientation and enrollment did not help the situation. The orientation professor was telling the doctor about the reaction he had had to some medication that the doctor had given him; meanwhile, when the professor attempted to sign the enrollment applications, his hand was trembling and shaking so badly that he could hardly sign them. He asked the doctor what was in the medication that he had given him. Frank and I just looked at each other in disbelief at what we were witnessing.

For the next couple of days, I tried to adjust to my new surroundings and way of life. Nevertheless, something just wasn't right. Nothing seemed to say, "Stay!" But everything seemed to say, "Go," even from the other students and professors. Others seemed to approach us as outsiders. The food and sleeping quarters of this Army barracks atmosphere didn't help. It was like there was something saying to me, "This is not the place for you; leave now before it's too late!" It was as if a sixth sense wanted me to move on. After only one week, and without making a friend or seeing anyone from the coaching staff, I and Frank decided to end our relationship with Natchez Junior College! Now! Here I was out of Oakland and out of Natchez Junior College. So where were the next steps in life going to take me? Still longing to be back in Oakland instead of Mississippi and those treacherous streets of Chicago, I believe subconsciously I knew better, based on the experiences I had.

Leaving Natchez Junior College I can say was a blessing from God because within weeks after I returned to my uncle and aunt's home at Anchor Curve, coach Woolfolk had arranged for me to receive a scholarship to Coahoma Junior College in Clarksdale, Mississippi. There I met and befriended students and basketball players from Greensboro, North Carolina; Bastrop, Louisiana; Tula, Mississippi; Paducah, Kentucky; and of course, Coahoma Junior Collage local Aggie high schools. They embraced me as I embraced them. Even to this day, I still have pleasant memories of them and the times we spent together as teammates and friends. For the first time in my academic studies, I was in the presence of teachers and administrators whose focus was career-oriented and required the same for all their students, no matter who we were or where we were from. The coaching staff was one of great inspiration, determination and leadership, with a strong emphasis on winning championships. That came with extreme tactics like four o'clock a.m. rousing wakeup for practices, banging on our walls and doors for the dreaded "19-59" or the "stogie cigar" long-distance runs.

Coach Gains and his assistants would come to our dormitory at four or five o'clock a.m., or any other early morning hour, when he felt like having practice. Then he would say, "**Men!** *Nineteen fifty-nine was a good year!*" We knew what that meant! Coach would then say **"Men! You see what a nice guy I am! I gave you a whole second off the twenty-minute-a-half game clock, wasn't that good of me?"** And we had to answer, "**Yes, Coach"** for building team camaraderie! The nineteen minutes and fifty-nine second run around the inside of our entire gym without stopping would officially start practices. This entailed running up one side of the bleacher rows to the top row, to the other end of that same row and then down that side to the court, to the other side of the gym, up that side of the bleachers to the top row of that side and down to the court. We had to repeat that process until the clock reached double zero, representing the first half of play. If anyone stopped or was caught loafing, we all had to repeat that same process by starting over.

Then there were the *stogie cigar runs* with the same repetition of the gym bleachers as the "19-59" run but without a definite time limit. The *stogie cigar run* did not depend on a certain time factor. It depended solely on how long it took coach to smoke up that stogie! Sometimes, if he was in a good mood, he would puff on it as if it were a freight train huffing and puffing, as he would blow the ashes off the end. And it would take him less than the *nineteen minutes and fifty nine second* run time frame to finish it. On other occasions, he would light that stogie, take a couple of puffs, lay it down and just walk away leaving it to burn, knowing that it would eventually go out, and we would run and run and run until he decided to light it up again. Some days, it would require him relighting it several times before he would finish smoking it, which could take up to an hour or longer. Now for many of the newcomers, as I was, this was our last chance for an education or any hope of playing the game we so dearly loved at that level or any hope of possibly advancing to the next levels, a major college, university or the NBA. Yes, I said the NBA. I truly believed I would reach that level of play!

I, like many others, were left with no other choice but to deal with Coach's style of coaching in order to remain in school to continue working toward achieving our goals in life. I could not afford the tuition nor could my mother or any of my family members. I, like many other student athletes in the same predicaments, was left with only one choice if we were to remain in school: stay and take his extreme coaching methods. I'm not saying that this is why Coach worked us so hard and that some of his coaching methods were questionable or improper. It was his way and method of preparing his players to win the achievable goals–Championships!

At other times, it seemed he was trying to weed out those who didn't have the will to win by making them cut or eliminate themselves by not being able to withstand the methodology of his practices. And I must say that many did crumble under his tough regime of running practices. And many nights I, too, contemplated leaving the team, but where would I go, back to Oakland or the cotton fields of Anchor Curve? At that time, I had no other choice but to stay and tough it out like the other newcomers; the Williamson brothers from Greensboro, North Carolina, and Prince, from Paducah, Kentucky. We stuck it out, as did a few before us, mostly the local players who knew what to expect; Tommy Jones, Raft

Walker and James "Wash" Washington. I could understand why so many would leave, especially those who had not been exposed to a hard-knock coaching style. Fortunately for me, I had been exposed through Coach Woolfolk, which contributed to me being able to withstand Coach Gain's unconventional coaching style. So I had to be physically and mentally strong in order to survive in my new surroundings and not let the severity of the coaching style force me out of school and back into an environment that encompassed a false lifestyle similar to the one I led in Oakland.

Nevertheless, Oakland was still in the picture. I was still having withdrawals from Oakland night life, and my midterm grades were at the point that made me a good candidate for academic probation status. I really needed some help. I did not know whom I could turn to for the help I so desperately needed without revealing the embarrassment that I only possessed the reading, writing and comprehension skills of possibly a freshman in high school. Even though I had made great progress in improving my academics skills my junior and senior years in high school, they were now in need of some fine tuning due to my engagement in a nonacademic lifestyle in Oakland. Quite naturally, this caused my academic skills to decline to where they were before high school, and the old adage applied: "if you don't *use it,* you will *lose it*" took center stage in my academic status.

Now fighting to survive academically and scholastically to compete for that elusive spot not only in the starting five but to remain in school, where could I turn for help? What a merry-go-round lifestyle I had placed myself in, and was there a jumping off place? Or maybe this whirlwind lifestyle of mine is all I would ever accomplish. Many nights, as in high school, I would lie awake asking myself when will it all end, or how could I end this vicious circle without totally embarrassing myself? Maybe I should be back at Anchor Curve in the cotton fields; they did not require an academic foundation, just enduring hard labor, something I was accustomed to since an early age, working hard in the cotton fields of Mississippi, the steel mill in Chicago, and later on, the assembly line at Del Monte Foods in Oakland.

So for that desperately needed help, I thought about talking with Coach but was terrified of losing my spot on the team. He had plans for me being the starting forward the upcoming season. The starting forward, Wash, had suffered a severe cut to his right eye by his jealous girlfriend and possibly wouldn't be able to play. Therefore, if I failed any of my classes, I would still lose that starting spot by being academically ineligible and possibly out of school. After much consideration, I thought of what Mom would always say: "trust in the Lord. He will make a way." She had always taught us not to rely on man or someone else for help. They all have good intentions but will fail you. God would lead me through these obstacles that were obstructing my academic and athletic needs. However, the one thing I kept letting elude me was that I must do God's will and not my own. And doing my will had already placed me in the same predicament I was in back in elementary and pre-high school, academically unprepared! My main focus was on other things; living the life of Riley—*an easy and pleasant life*, by conjuring up unrealistic things and ideas that dealt with sports achievement and goals I couldn't accomplish without academics. I was not putting in the time and effort that was necessary to accomplish my goals.

For the remainder of that first semester I spent all of my time in some kind of isolation in order to be able to reconnect with my faith and concentrate on my academics, by making sure I understood just what my professors' lesson plans required of me. I had to read things numerous times to get its meaning. Many nights and days I spent defining words to improve my vocabulary and to be able to read and write better, with proficiency being my goal. By employing this rigid study habit and schedule, as Coach had employed his tough practice schedule, I was able to compete academically and keep my scholarship and maintain my spot on the team. Just like Mom always said: "success comes from hard work and to never giving up, to persevere." Perseverance and diligence paid off not only in the cotton fields but also in life, academia and sports! I really began to understand just what she meant, that whatever my aspirations were in life, to accomplish them I must not only employ hard work but more importantly include God to obtain my true goals.

At the end of my second year and a few credits short of graduating from Coahoma Junior College in 1971, I found myself back in Chicago with Mom and my two younger brothers. Mom's health had started to fail her from the many years she had to slave away in Mississippi while cooking and caring for us, and working for those demanding plantation owners who required her services of cooking, cleaning and catering to them and their children's every need. Then she worked those long hours at that Westside soul food restaurant in its sizzling hot kitchens. It all had taken a toll on her. For all of her efforts, she had only the shame of being a welfare recipient to show for it all. I felt totally responsible for Mom having to work all those years.

So the compelling question was...

Had I finally learned my lesson of what a life without God in the picture can lead to?

Chapter 15

BACK TO CHICAGO

Proverbs 25:28: "Whoever has no rule over his' own Spirit; is like a city broken down, without walls."

Six years had passed since I entered downtown Chicago on a Greyhound bus. It was much different than the summer of 1966. This time, I had some idea of what to expect and was not as overwhelmed and captivated. Even though I had seen it all before I still was somewhat amazed and looking forward to the ride from the bus station to where Mom, Jessie and James were now living, on West Washington Boulevard. I had some general ideas of what to expect from the neighborhood since I had spent a summer near there with Sim six years earlier. How much could have changed since 1966?

When Mom and my two brothers Jessie and James first moved to Chicago, they had to live with her youngest sister, Aunt Betty, and her family of four. Like many other undereducated ex-Mississippians who had moved north to escape the harsh conditions associated with share-cropping, they were forced to seek residence in some of Chicago's most impoverished communities. For them, it was the twenty-six hundred block of Poke Street on Chicago's southwest side. Most of that surrounding community was riddled with mischief; gang warfare, drugs and prostitution were a daily occurrence. All its clientele were trying so desperately to carve a living out of their difficult living conditions. There was so much danger there and lost HOPE because of the gamesmanship and maneuvering done by a few just to earn insufficient bucks to feed their "Jones," that next fix to relieve their pains if only for a short period of time before that vicious addictive cycle would need feeding again. I was grateful that I didn't have to move to Poke Street; West Washington was much better.

I could see clearly for the first time how easy it was going to be to get back into what I evolved into when I was in Oakland. I had done so well at Coahoma, and now I risked backsliding. Seeing Mom struggle with her health as she continually tried to work at that hot soul food restaurant kitchen was heartbreaking. I knew that I had let her down even though she would never admit it; that's the kind of woman and mother she was. I also knew that God had given me another opportunity to help care for Mom. He saved me from Oakland's menacing streets by the way of Natchez and Coahoma and finally placed me back in Chicago with Mom. This gave me an opportunity to remove Mom out of the intense working conditions, and I took full advantage of this new opportunity. My sister, Lueretha, cared for Mom's daily needs while caring for her own family. I worked whatever legal odd jobs I could find. Mom would never accept any money or anything that came from any illegal sources or activities to pay her bills, so she didn't have to work anymore. She could now relax and do the things that were important to her; mostly talking on the phone with her friends to catch up with what was going on in Louise and Greeneville, Mississippi, and having nice clothing and a few pieces of jewelry that she never had back in Mississippi.

My first full-time job after being back in Chicago was with Curtis Candy Company in its shipping and receiving department, in a northwestern suburb of Chicago. This job required me to be a part of a car pool in lieu of public transportation, and I didn't have a car or money to buy one at that time. Being a part of that car pool required me to be up and ready to leave home at six o'clock a.m. each day. I worked from eight a.m. to four p.m. Monday through Friday. This work environment involved some of the most underhanded methods of manipulation you could imagine for advancement into a less strenuous demanding position. Working on the assembly lines handling a continuous flow of boxes filled with candy moving down a conveyor belt was extremely taxing and exhausting. Belt! Those words still bring back awful memories of my corporal punishment beatings back in elementary school. Now I was taking another kind of beating from a conveyor belt. This time it was from the daily ritual of catching and stacking cases of candy and peanut-filled boxes on pallets four tiers high with an interlocking pattern, a job ONLY for the uneducated. *RIGHT!* Those tireless working conditions required me to catch those cases, weighing anywhere from ten to fifty pounds, that were being propelled at me down that fast-moving belt. Once

I had caught one, I had to make a quick turn to my left or right, all depending on which side of the pallet I was working from and neatly stack it matching the footprint of the pallet without any overhang. At the same time, another propelled down the belt. With each stacking scenario, there was continuous stress and demanding movement placed on my back. This type of backbreaking work reminded me of the cotton picking rituals.

In order for me to perform this box-stacking task, I had to go through a short box-stacking training session. My box-stacking training sessions and its methodology focused mainly on eliminating edge-hanging problems and not injury prevention. The slightest edge overhang would ruin the structural soundness of the cube design, impeding the forklift driver's pallet stacking blueprint. Obviously, perfecting the pallet's outline was more important than health and well-being. The major concerns were placed on making ideal pallets for them to fit properly into trucks for shipments, long and short distance. So great demands were placed on building high-quality and solid cubes to eliminate any problems with loading and unloading. This demanding job only paid the minimum wage of $1.60 per hour. But considering that picking cotton paid $0.05 per pound and cultivating (chopping, weeding) was $0.30 per hour, I guess I shouldn't complain!

After taxes, my take-home pay for a forty hour week was a whopping FIFTY ONE DOLLARS AND TWENTY CENTS. Ten of those dollars each week went for my car pooling expense. It seemed kind of steep that anyone would charge ten dollars for carpooling when we all knew each other. Walter was going that way anyway. But that was his decision, and if I wanted to keep my job I had to pay his price, since he was my only ride. I'm not saying that he shouldn't have been compensated for giving me a ride, but ten dollars a week for gas from four friends seemed steep, with gas at $0.36 to $0.40 per gallon.

I was employed at Curtis Candy Company for approximately a year and half. And during my employment I also encountered other forms of the most manipulative, wicked, and boldest individuals I had ever met and hoped to never have to meet again in my lifetime. These individuals would steal merchandises from different department stores, ranging from color television sets to all different kinds of shoes, clothing for adults, children and babies; watches, rings and food stamps. If you wanted it and they didn't have it, they would get it for you. During our lunch times, that were broken down into three thirty-minute lunch slots between 11:30 a.m. and ended at 1:00 p.m., depending on your shift, these Con Artists, or mobile merchants, mainly from Chicago's Westside, would be open for business in the parking lot, especially Fridays on pay day! Then the gamesmanship would begin!

These mobile merchants would set up their mini flea markets in the parking lot and operate right from the trunks of their cars. These peddlers peddled their stolen merchandise for money to purchase more drugs. They were some of the craftiest, cunning and shrewdest bunch I had ever seen operate. I tried to avoid their shady ways of gamesmanship and deceitfulness associated with the purchasing frenzy linked to their mini flea market. But like the others I, too, fell prey to their con. I wanted to purchase a color television set for my mom to make her retirement complete. Two guys that lived in my neighborhood and were members of the mini flee market brigade said they had just what I was looking for; those words *just what I was looking for* should have been a red flag for me to not purchase that new RCA color television set they had in the trunk of their car. It appeared to have never been taken out of its box, listing all the features of an RCA color television set. They even opened the box and showed me the front of what was to be our new color television. As they took that alleged television set out of the trunk of their car and placed it in the trunk of the car I pooled in, they displayed a royal performance fit for any Hollywood set. As they pretended to struggle mightily in their effort to remove and transport a heavy television set out of the trunk of their car and place it into the trunk of the pool car. They closed the trunk, collected fifty of my hard-earned dollars for an award-winning performance and casually walked over to their car, got in and drove off.

Our lunch time was over and I along with the other flea market shoppers returned to work. For the remaining of my afternoon shift, four o' clock seemed to take forever. I couldn't wait to show Mom her new color television set. Routinely on Friday after work, we all would meet in the parking lot to figure out what we were going to do that night or over the weekend. Once our meeting was over, one of my best friends, Caleb, asked to see the new color television. Thank God and Christ that he did! Because when I opened the trunk of the car and I reached inside and moved the box to open it, it was as light as one of those small boxes of packed peanuts. I knew then that I had been ripped off, made a fool of, conned! What they had sold me was a royal performance because that was the only thing I got for my money. The box that allegedly had a color television set in it turned out to be nothing but a television set shell without any of its internal parts. So several of the guys suggested that we go and take back my money followed by giving those con artists a royal... kicking.

Of course I said no, not because I was afraid or worried about the repercussions but because I knew that was the last thing Mom would want me to be involved in, violence! So I swallowed my pride and moved on with trying to define my life and let God judge them. And each time after that scam that I saw them, I pretended not to recognize the artists and just made sure that I would not be conned again by them or anyone!

So to say the least I was home that Friday night and not hanging out at our usual place, Bob's Liquor store, or a house party. There were always places to go or something to do. I just wasn't in the mood to be around anyone. I was trying to figure out why anyone would go to all that trouble to con someone out of fifty dollars. Was the time and effort worth it to possibly risk some major consequences or even their lives? I guess it was for someone like them—the wicked, lazy and freeloaders. For weeks, I kept asking myself how I could have been so stupid to let this happen to me. Wasn't I street smart enough to see it coming? Did I have sucker written across my forehead? Or didn't I learn anything from the streets of Oakland that would help me compete with the poverty-stricken. Wicked and unprosperous souls who sought pleasure by conning their way through life? Totally vanity!

Working Closer to Home

With no regrets, I left the Curtis Candy Company assembly line to work at Bob's Liquor and Sundries. Even though I was making less money, my clerking job at Bob's was only three blocks away from home. Our home on West Washington was actually a second floor walkup, one bedroom apartment that the four of us shared: Mom, Jessie, James and me. It was in a courtyard building in a community that wasn't yet infested with crime, drugs, street gangs, and prostitution but had its share of mice and rats as big as young kittens; and to top it off, cockroaches! We had to live in this type of community since we were the undereducated, the welfare recipients, and the working poor and even lower than the house poor. But we still had something that other didn't: love of a great woman! She insisted that we keep everything clean just as she had demanded of us back in Mississippi, down to sweeping the dirt in our front yard! Mom also consistently demanded that the landlord spray insecticide to control the pests that ran from apartment to apartment to escape extermination.

Chapter 16

CONTINUOUS LIES AND THEIR CONSEQUENCES

1 John 2:15-17: "The whole world system is built on pride, lust, ego, materialism, vanity, and emptiness."

W hile working at the liquor store, I lost control of my spirit once again instead of helping take care of Mom. I let myself be tripped up by the things I was seeing. I didn't adhere to the spirit inside that was trying so desperately to lead me by faith and not by sight, as it so clearly states in *II Corinthian 5:7: "we walk by faith not by sight."* For example, I had concealed my stash of marijuana in our apartment in one of Mom's decorative head figures hanging on the wall in the living room. When I went back to retrieve it, it wasn't there, Mom was waiting for me and said that she had flushed it down the toilet! After licking my wounds and having had my stash flushed down the toilet, I was back out there once again at my usual hot spot on one of the neighborhood basket-ball courts, waiting for my turn and looking to score some more weed.

Then I started to think about how I had let myself revert into my old lifestyle after making such great prog-ress at Coahoma Junior College. Now since I had relapsed into my sinful ways, had this made me any different from those con artists? In the eyes of GOD, a sin is a sin, and I had let myself get involved in immoral things again. So what made me any different from them? We all were committing sins against the body of Christ. Therefore, if my sins were using drugs, alcohol and worshiping NBA and NFL stars, who was I to cast ill will or pass judgment upon other sinners, regardless of their sins?

John 8:1-11… Speaks of a woman that was caught in an adulterous act and the Pharisees and religious leaders were going to stone her to death. The act they wanted to perform represented the height of self-righteousness and hypocrisy. *Jesus revealed to them that their inner hearts were as sinful as her act of adultery. Jesus* did not condemn her for her sins. Rather, He offered up to her forgiveness and restoration. *Jesus* did not approve of her sins and *He* told her so *"not to sin no more." Jesus'* approach was one of an "Agape Love" and not one of self-righteousness like the Pharisees.

Now the compelling question is…

Could these verses be the reasons why I didn't retal-iate against those con artists? For whatever reasons, I still did not want to relinquish the control of my life to God and Christ. And He never forced me to surrender that control to Him nor His son, Jesus. However, during my fall from Their Grace, I knew that God and Christ still had Their Hands on me and that is why I was so forgiving and had such a contrite heart even for those who had wronged me. Even though I vowed not to let anyone con me again, I knew that I was going to be scammed, in some form or fashion, as long as I continued to walk by sight.

For the next four years, I did have to live on the Westside of the Windy City, surrounded by conmen, and I served many of them at Bob's Liquor for two of those four years before enrolling in Aurora College the fall of 1972. As predicted, I was cheated more times than I care to remember, by some who called themselves my friends and by individuals I met through those so-called friends. To my surprise, they (males, females, including a few family members) thought they weren't doing anything wrong. I was just another sucker or mark, and this was another part of that culture with which I had to deal. So I would tell myself that they weren't hurting me as long as I knew what they were up to. I know this sounds impractical, but I just wanted to fit in as if this were some kind of ongoing initiation into their impoverished social club or fraternity. I had let my immoral ways hide my Christian faith, and I was more than willing to distort that upbringing to be accepted. Like me, many others within our social groups were unable to stop the feeding frenzies, daily and nightly diet of self-pleasure. I became so captivated by the materialistic misdeeds of those around me that I started looking for that one big perfect score or opportunity, not for the glory of God but mine (Pride).

So to say the least, I was weakening my integrity while ignoring the Holy Spirit. Smoking marijuana had become a daily ritual while cruising the streets of Chicago looking and lusting for the things that my flesh was craving (Oakland all over again), to help me forget my inability to achieve greatness and the miseries of how we were living. I had let my corrupted environment rip away all the good morals and values I was taught as a child. *I had been deceived and let evil corrupt my good habits 1 Corinthians 15:33.* As it says in *1 Corinthians 15:34 "Awake to righteousness, and do not sin…"*

So the next compelling questions became, is there Hope for a "Coward" in Christ's Kingdom…?

I was, as predicted by my teacher, destined to become Nobody. I would get up early in the morning and take a bus downtown to State Street. I walked around until I was certain that no one knew me and saw me entering adult movie theaters. I was there to watch women on the big screen instead of the 8mm films that I watched in Oakland. I definitely wasn't there to meet anyone. I only wanted to be invisible while watching my favorite female adult entertainers. My secret lifestyle was a nerve-racking experience. I was scrutinizing those adult establishments like bank robbers would check out a bank before entering it.

I finally accepted that I had a serious problem and needed help to overcome it. My slow repentance started again the summer of 1972, my last year in Chicago and working at Bob's Liquor Store. I worked from 6:00 p.m. until 2:00 a.m. Bob's was the focal point of our community, which was anchored by Austin Avenue to the west, Cicero Avenue to the east, Lake Street to the north and Jackson Street to the south. Although I often saw the dregs of society, I also saw some of the most dazzling and intelligent accomplishments of young women and men; they had success written all over their faces. However, within months some of them had turned into accomplices, the captivating street life had taken them hostage, as it had me, into its vicious circle of mediocrity and self-fulfillment with no way out.

I came to realize that working at Bob's Liquor Store was a blessing in disguise. I initially thought that it gave me the opportunity to carry out my mysterious Dr. Jekyll and Mr. Hyde persona. But to the contrary, it gave me a vision into the future to see what life had in store for me if I didn't change my ways. My job at Bob's had given me the opportunity to see firsthand just what I was destined to become, in the eyes and faces of those that came each night: the accomplices, the players and pimps; the con artists and hustlers and their groupies; drug addicts and alcoholics. I could see myself in them doing whatever it took to help satisfy their craving or to ease their troubled existent. We all had that same monkey on our backs, an immoral craving that needed to be fed.

An Awakening

Since God's word says *the LORD shall make thee the head, and not the tail; and thou shalt be above only, and thou shalt not be beneath; if that thou hearken unto the commandments of the LORD thy God, which*

I command thee this day, to observe and to do them, Deuteronomy 28:13.

How ironic that the help I so desperately needed to overcome my addictions to marijuana and adult entertainment, God provided from the same source that started it, the game I once loved so dearly, basketball. Finally, I was back playing basketball, and its social group accepted me for my God-given ability to play the game. I made new friends through basketball, including a few professional athletes, and this helped me to refocus and somewhat ease my pains but didn't cure them; still, this meant a great deal to me. After pickup, league, or tournament games were over, I went my way and they went theirs. Even though only a few of the guys ever visited where I lived or seemed to have any desire or inclination to do so, that was okay too. It gave me something positive to build on. I heartily accepted that type of athletic befriending for whatever it was worth, even if it meant that I only associated with the majority of them at athletic events. I knew that I was from another socioeconomic class and our one bedroom apartment wasn't suitable for entertaining.

I continued to work nights and weekends at Bob's, but he gave me time off when I needed it in order to play basketball in the Chicago Catholic Youth Organization, CYO league. I played with Caleb Glover, Fuzzy O'Neal, James Stewart, Tom Harris and Earl Rogers (our player manager) and we won the 1972 CYO league championship. Also, I couldn't believe that I got the opportunity to play with and against some of Chicago's greatest professionals, universities, colleges, and playground legends that would emerge to play in the Boys and Girls Club Summer League tournament.

For me, this would be an education in itself to play with guys who had such a great and true love for the game of basketball. To prepare for this new possible opportunity, I understood that I needed to improve my game. I had to develop a reputation that I, too, had "Game" and could play with the best that Chicago had to offer. I, along with a few of my CYO league members and friends, Caleb, Fuzzy, Earl and Jud Jones, would ride our bicycles all over Chicago to play in pickup games, "street basketball," to keep our game razor sharp for the Columbus Park tournament, operated by Danny Crawford, that was followed by the Boys and Girls Club Summer League Classic tournament.

By far the greatest unorganized competition that one could find at that time was at the old Navy Pier gymnasium. The games were played using the following rules and scoring methodology: you called your own fouls; no free throws were awarded or taken; scoring was progressive – "make it, take it" (meaning if your team scored your team kept the ball); play to eleven points by one (each basket scored counted as a single point). This process was continued until the first team reached eleven points and had to win by two points. It seemed like hundreds of players would emerge at Navy Pier from all over Chicago to play in those "four against four," half-court games on six to eight courts.

Teams were typically picked by players who had the highest status according to competition levels. It was similar to how the National Collegiate Athletic Association (NCAA) and National Invitation Tournament (NIT) teams are selected. The NCAA tournament selection committee usually selects teams with the best winning records or best match up status, not necessarily the high-market teams. Those that don't make the NCAA's cut "to attend the big dance," as it is called, go to the NIT tournament, which is played in New York at Madison Square Garden. Generally, the NCAA tournaments are more popular and played at various high-profile arenas. Therefore, the Navy Pier pickup games became the more popular place to play in hopes of being selected to play in a replica NCAA tournament at the Boys and Girls Club or a Columbus Park NIT tournament replica.

From my play in the Columbus Park pickup games and tournaments, as well as Navy Pier pickup games, I was able to display my talents to be selected as a substitute player with the elitist at the Boys and Girls Club with NBA's Chicago Bulls players–Bob "Butterbean" Love; we (myself and Robert Scott) use to go to his home in Rolling Meadows to play ball. We played against other great Summer League teams that featured DePaul University & NBA greats – Mark Aguirre and Terry Cummings; Texas A&M University & NBA great Sonny Parker; Aurora College & NBA great Mickey Johnson; other great players from Aurora College – Edward "Bad News" Bonner; playground legends Caleb Glover, Fuzzy O'Neal, Tom Harris, Robert Scott, Paul, Steve, Blue, Money Mondane, Ernest "Fats" Jones, and Jud Jones. Then, last but not least were Earl Rogers and Columbus Park tournament organizer, grad of Northeastern Illinois University and now NBA Official – Danny Crawford.

Playing in those unorganized pickup games at Navy Pier, the pickup and organized games at Columbus Park and the elite games of the Boys and Girls Club tournaments helped me to better understand why Mom, my two brothers and I, along with so many other individuals, had to live in the ghetto. We were undereducated. We were the NIT players in life, unprepared academically to compete with the NCAA and the NBA-educated elitist players in the job markets.

When I did rely on my own mortal abilities for help defining my life goals, I always fell short. I had to learn that hard work alone wasn't enough to achieve my goals in life. I had to continue to repent of my sins to perfect my God-given talent. I also had to realize that spiritual gifts are available to anyone who believes in Christ, even today. But God does not always give each person all or the same gifts. And most importantly, I had to give up those things that were holding me back. I was being deceived by the corrupt company I had been keeping, which changed my good habits and the desire for a good education. Not only did I have to educate myself to this new style of playing basketball, I had to develop my other gifts and talents I needed to accomplish the task at hand. I had to not only repent of my sins but start believing *IN* God and His word by *FAITH* instead of just believing there is a God.

So I ask myself this important question:
How significant is an education to my successes
or failures in life?

Quite naturally, I received two answers to my request, as with any question, one being that of man's earthly wisdom and the other one that of growing to accept and believe in Christ's Wisdom, which is spiritual, as my Lord and Savior. My earthly wisdom tried to tell me that furthering my education was not important to achieve my goals in life. I already had a high school diploma and two years of junior college. All I needed to do was work hard to achieve my successes in life; is this vanity? My earthly wisdom kept reminding me of the suffering I had to deal with in pursuits academically. My Spiritual Wisdom helped me to focus and realize just how important continuing education really was; and without it, how could I continue to read and understand what God's word says and what it takes to achieve His glory in my life?

Therefore! If education wasn't vital to one's successes in life, why, then, did slave and plantation owners enslave those who could not read nor write their language and then prohibit them from being acclimated or educated in their origins? Being a close relative of many who were a part of the Great Migration north, 1914 – 1950, I felt that I was looked upon as an expendable student that could be sacrificed in lieu of my suburban counterparts. Much later in life, as a counselor at the Illinois Youth Correctional facility, and the founder/director/mentor of Family Advocacy Mentoring, Inc., (FAM) an after-school educational mentoring and tutoring program. I learned there were many other students who felt the same *lost hope* of being expendable, as I did. I also learned from researching my roots that many of those expendable students' ancestors, like mine, had contributed greatly to the success of this country.

They had taken those jobs that didn't require an education and initially I followed in their footsteps. Into a lifestyle that was much easier than being accepted into a suburban community and their state of art schools, which contained all the key ingredients needed to help a student like me to succeed in life. Don't take this the wrong way; I'm not saying that all the students who attended those state of the art suburban schools are going to achieve greatness in life. Nor am I saying that all urban and rural disadvantaged schools produce failures. What I'm saying is that I felt that each child should have had the same opportunities to obtain a quality education. In God's eyes, we all should share the same opportunities in life to success and with God on our side who can be against us!

However, without those key academic tools, it limited my proficiency to not only understand what God's word said but delayed me from graduating high school two years and college for three decades, what a waste. I felt that those squandered early educational foundation opportunities led directly to my addictions. Therefore, I ended up only hurting my integrity more than using it positively to help Mom and others. More importantly now I know that those fruitless years had a direct negative effect to my God-given talent as a sower. However, in my sober mind I knew that education meant emancipation and sovereignty, but my addictive nature led me to believe that I could obtain life's success without an education through sports or craftiness. What a lie!

Chapter 17

LEAVING CHICAGO'S PSEUDO-SOPHISTICATION

Hebrews 3:19: "They could not enter because of unbelief."

Sophomore Year

From my first visit in August 1975, I fell in love with Aurora College's small, quaint and pleasant surroundings and its impeccable campus. In my attempt to leave Chicago's pseudo-sophistication behind me, I enrolled in Aurora College, Aurora, Illinois, in September 1975. The credits I earned from Coahoma Junior College, Clarksdale,

Mississippi, allowed me to enter as a second-term sophomore, with plans to graduate in two and half years.

Of course, coming from the environment that I did, at first I did not apply myself academically. And there were a few athletes who were more than willing to help me in my diversion from my classroom responsibilities with coercing parties. They were concocted and carried out by a few veteran players to rid themselves of the incoming competition. I fell for their conniving scheme, not realizing that I was not the only one there with the aspiration of playing at the next level, a professional athletic. Once again, I had let the father of lies' craftiness lure me into another drugs and alcohol subculture. This time, I had fallen prey to the so-called fun times of college life in the 70s!

There, I also met instructors who did not care about athletic abilities or how good you were at playing sports—academics came first. Even though I still went to class, I wasn't prepared academically, and eventually that led to academic probation my first semester. To top that off, the head coach, Jack Augustine, had a problem with my apparel! Dungarees, as he referred to them, didn't fit his dress code. He demanded that his players wear dress slacks or khakis. So since the only slacks I owned were blue jeans, I was only allowed to participate in home games but was unable to travel with the team. He also did not like my aggressive street style of run-and-shoot basketball. That following summer, I landed a job working for an outreach family program. I earned enough money to purchase the proper attire to be able to participate in the away games. I also worked on toning down my street style of play to fit into Coach's system, which consisted of slower play passing the ball at least five time before each shot.

To test Coach Augustine's new coaching philosophy, we took it on the road; back to Chicago's Westside and entered the Columbus Park basketball Summer League tournament. To say the least, we were run out of the gym, totally outclassed. We'd lost by large double figures in the first and second rounds and were out of the tournament. Following that embarrassing experience in a league where I once was a noted player, coupled with my first year experience in playing for Coach Augustine, I thought those two incidents had prepared me for anything he could throw at me. I was wrong. My next experience left me wondering what had I gotten myself into and was there any way out. Or how could I continue to play basketball for a coach who had an incredible dislike for me and my style of playing? As if I had harmed him in another life.

Realizing that this was the only means for me to remain in school, I had no choice but to play his way and do whatever he said. I had to reach back to my experience of how I handled Coach "Pop" Gain's dreaded stogie cigar and nineteen-fifty-nine runs to find the strength God had given me then to endure Coach Augustine. Over the next year and a half, I played the game the way Coach wanted, even though we seldom won a game. Coach's attitude toward me didn't change, even with me conforming to his every request. He always seemed to look for something to punish me for by not letting me play until we were behind in points and there was no way we could catch up. It was as if this was his way of blaming me for those losses.

Home Game

One game in particular his dislike for me came out loud and clear; and even more shocking, not one of my teammates stepped in on my behalf. I was falsely accused of doing something I didn't do, and they knew I was innocent. At an away game during our regular warm up drills (Coach Augustine and the officiating crew were standing by the scorer's table). Ed, one of my teammates was in front of me and attempted to dunk the basketball knowing that dunking was not allowed in those days. He missed the dunk, slamming the basketball against the back of the rim and the backboard causing a thunderous sound. Coach Augustine and the officiating crew immediately turned and saw me underneath the basketball hoop. The officials proceeded to assess me with a technical foul without seeing who attempted the dunk. The officials and my coach assumed it was me. Immediately, Coach

Augustine called me over and scolded me, "I told you not to dunk the basketball," even before I could say anything in my defense. He just wanted it to be me without even assuming that it could have been one of my teammates that had attempted that dunk. He then proceeded to discipline me by not letting me play in any of the games during that tournament. I learned a vital lesson from that incident – there was nothing I could ever do or say to please Coach, and of the twelve other players on my team, not one stepped up in my defense, to say "Coach, Joe didn't do it!" They all knew who had attempted the dunk.

Even to this day it sometimes troubles me why not even one of those guys, especially my roommate, didn't step up and say "Coach, Joe wasn't the one who attempted that dunk." I thought we had formed some kind of brotherhood bond together. What were their motives? Why did all of them keep quiet! Would it have made a difference if anyone had stepped up on my behalf? Or was it competitive aspirations motivated?

Maybe it was due to my new friend, Lisa Hall, a model who did not return for her sophomore year as she took her modeling career on the road both nationally and internationally. I believed that most of the other guys on campus would have given almost anything to be with her. She befriended me, I befriended her and it was a kind of friendship, like we had known each other in another life. Though she was used to getting anything she wanted, with everyone catering to her every need. However, we had many magnificent adventures together nationally and internationally, and a tie was formed, uniting us together for life. She is a very good friend of the family, and my wife and she, to this day, have created a bond, as well.

Her oldest son, Gavin, and I share the same birthday and love of basketball; he now plays for the Michigan State Spartan! Her son Nigel is an outstanding piano player, illusionist and soccer player who can charm anyone.

The continued unnecessary hurtful treatment helped me to make a hard decision that I had been contemplating. I knew now that I had to leave the team and never return. This meant getting my own place! My senior year, I applied for financial aid and received it because of Mom's and my financial status. Now I was able to turn all my attention toward graduation. With just one semester to complete, which consisted of an internship to fulfill my graduation requirements, spring semester of 1978, I was able to fulfill that requirement at St. Charles Illinois Youth Center (IYC) (*Charlie Town, as staff and inmates referred to it*), a level 2 medium-security facility.

Also, while playing for Aurora College, I attended one of Mickey's summer basketball camps with former NBA star players with the Chicago Bulls and Coach for the Utah Jazz, Jerry Sloan. In spite of all the controversy that took place between Coach Augustine and myself, and even after leaving the team my senior year, I truly believed that with the contacts I had created I was on my way to a career in professional basketball. However, with that belief, I placed myself back in the same situation I had been in numerous times before, academically unprepared and making it extremely difficult to keep up scholastically. But with the assistance of Assistant Professor Rayonia Babel—"Ray" as she preferred to be called her—a beloved friend who mentored and tutored me, I was finally able to graduate from Aurora College in June of 1978 with a degree in Criminal Justice.

The summer after graduation, while playing in a pickup game on campus to keep my skills sharp, I sustained a serious knee injury. I tore my patella tendon and dislocated my kneecap; this changed my life plan of becoming a professional athlete! Due to the difficultly in recovering from a serious knee injury such as mine back then, my professional basketball career was in serious jeopardy of being over, if not over. I had no other choice but to try to find a job with my degree. Fortunately, the mentoring and tutoring assistance I received from Ray and also Professor Tom Dull helped me learn how to channel my energy levels, to enjoy life, to accept what life had to offer. Most importantly, I learned from them to be a team player in all areas of life and not just in sports and to not let physical injuries or being the product of a primitive educational system define my goals in life.

Chapter 18

MY ADVENTURES AT CHARLIE TOWN

1 Corinthians 15:33 "Evil Company corrupts good habits."

I N FALL 1979, with degree in hand I was able to get a counseling job back at IYC, Charlie Town, after completing my internship there and working six months at IYC Valley View as a youth supervisor. From the many individuals I met through Aurora College, coworkers from IYC Charley Town and Valley View; from the City of Aurora itself, I befriended a few individuals with whom I thought I had formed a bond for life. We looked out for each other, shared stories of past and present adventures over a cold beer or two and went out to lunch almost every day together. Since I was the only single one, we gravitated to my house and watched basketball and football games together. Or occasionally we would go to one of the local bars after work on Fridays for happy hour, just to have something different to do.

I spent the next eleven and a half years at IYC St. Charles. There I worked as a Crisis Prevention and Intervention Counselor; the Chairperson of Youths Grievance and Adjustment Committee. In my role as a Crisis Prevention and Intervention Counselor, I worked with some of Illinois' most hardened juvenile offenders that also held adult status.

Most people, including some professionals, para-professionals, practitioners, and even some of our legal advisors, believed the words "counseling" or "at-risk and non-traditional adolescence" meant simply "under achievement." Yes, adolescents who are in need of counseling or mentoring or at-risk teens can be under-achievers, but I learned that's only the symptom for most part. My work at IYC St. Charles revealed their true problems are centered on survival itself. Ninety-five percent of the adolescents I counseled at IYC came from the poverty-stricken ghettos that I had once experienced. Many came from fractured families and high-crime neighborhoods where violence and drug abuse extend right into their homes. Then there were those who came from affluent families that had it all. One of the defining factors was a lack of love; an *"Agape love,"* which is Christ-like that maintains peace within the church that evolves into the family, friends and others. Unfortunately, the love that many of them found, as I had experienced, is not that *Agape love* that is found on the impoverished streets and communities of cities like urban Oakland and Chicago or like my rural town, Louise, Mississippi, juke joints had to offer.

I so desperately wanted to educate my clientele at IYC and later FAM's participants, along with their parents or legal guardian, that the love the Bible refers to in *Romans 5:5 (paraphrasing)* is not a love by chance or human emotion. *But* God's Agape love *"an undefeatable benevolence and unconquerable goodwill that always seeks the highest good of the other person, no matter what he or she does."* Even though I strayed from my upbringing, if these factors had not been addressed in my early and adolescent years by Mom and Grandma Retta, I can imagine where I would have ended up. Most likely, like the adolescents I would later counsel, thinking that I could only succeed at one thing…FAILURE.

From my countless clientele's case studies, I could see images of myself in many of them, of how I once, too, turned to someone for help who shared the same misery as I did. With those analogies, I was able to share with each one of my clients how important God's love was in turning my life around and could potentially change theirs. However, my regret was that I couldn't physically be there to help them when they were paroled, as many of them had no other choice but to return to those same dysfunctional families whose dependency on illegal activities, alcohol and other drug abuse offered little hope. It saddened me knowing that after being paroled many of them would end up in overcrowded, poorly-organized group or treatment homes and as a last resort reenter a correctional facility, *if death didn't intervene.* As I, too, had and would return to those who shared my same misery, I thank God every day that death didn't intervene to relieve my earthly pains.

Life's Bittersweet

As the Chairperson of the Youth Grievance Committee, which I enjoyed, I could make recommendations to influence or change the outcomes of disputes. I could ensure that the youth received reimbursement for lost or stolen property. I could launch an investigation into accusations of abuse and unlawful treatment. And as the Chairperson of the Adjustment Committee, alongside two other members I had the authority to reduce or extend an inmate's stay according to program requirements of behavior modification and guided group interaction. I also could make recommendation of the proper counseling and medication with approval from clinical services. There were numerous times we, the committee, had to extend an inmate's stay in the department due to negative or inappropriate behavior, even those cases where they were not properly supervised. As chairperson, I still had to hold each youthful offender accountable for their actions, as well, which was very difficult.

Driving 95 mph in my Datsun 280Z!

It was the summer of 1981. I was living on the ninth floor of an eleven floor high-rise in Aurora, and life appeared to be great for me. I decided to take a trip home to Mississippi to see my Aunt Pearly, Uncle Joe Willie and my few remaining friends. Although, my main motive was to show off my 1978 mint condition Datsun 280Z and my wealth to those who thought I was going to be just another sharecropper. I had finally matched my older brothers and had a really cool car! I packed a few belongings, along with some of my "stash" and was off to Mississippi to show off my bogus success. Self-importance!

As I look back over the way things transpired that week, I know that God had to be with me from the beginning and for sure throughout the end of my trip. Even before I left my Aurora apartment, I had smoked a joint. Then I got behind the wheel of my Datsun 280Z and was off to Mississippi. Once I was on interstate 55 South, headed to St. Louis, Missouri, I consumed more of my stash as my speed nearly exceeded triple digits until I reached highway 61 that took me through Memphis, Tennessee, south to the Mississippi Delta, reaching Anchor Curve in record time, without incidents as I only stopped for food and gas with an occasional bathroom break. Some fifteen hours later I had arrived at my Uncle and Aunt's home, unpacked and was off looking to show off my new toy and party. I partied several days with some friends in Yazoo City and a few nights at a semi-prestigious night-club called the Key Club. I then hung out in Louise and got reacquainted with my aunt and uncle. I hadn't seen them since I left Coahoma Junior College in 1970. But by the end of that week, Friday, my Mississippi vacation had become boring since my stash and money was running low, so I decided to head home. Early Saturday morning I was on the road home and about fifty miles south of St. Louis and I decided to smoke my last joint. To keep the residue off my fingertips when smoking, I always kept a pair of hemostat surgical scissor to hold my joints. After I had finished smoking that last joint I put the scissor in the center console pocket between the front seats and had about a half gram of cocaine left from the "sixteenth" I started the trip with. Now I was cruising at about 95 miles per hour going north on Interstate 55 about 30 miles from St. Louis, when I saw a state policeman going south. He immediately turned on his siren and flashing light then crossed the ditch and came after me!

Since I had smoked my last marijuana, I thought the only thing I had left to get rid of was the cocaine. So I slowed down and let down the passenger side window and threw it out of the car. As I pulled over to the side of the road and waited for him, I watched through the rear view mirror to see if he saw me toss the coke out of the car. He drove up behind me, got out of his car with hands on his gun and for some strange reason instead of coming to the driver side of the car, he went to the passenger side and opened the door and got in. He then proceeded to ask where I was coming from and where was I going to in such a hurry. I told him I had visited my aunt and uncle in Anchor Curve, Mississippi and I lived in Aurora, Illinois. Next, he instructed me to take everything out of my baggage piece by piece and turn the pockets inside out, and I did. When he asked to see my driver's license, I knew that I could be in some minor if not serious trouble. I kept my wallet in the center console pocket where the marijuana residue-tipped surgical scissor was kept. When I opened the center console he saw the scissor and told me to take it out. He asked me what I used them for *and not to lie* because he could have them tested. So of course I said to smoke marijuana. He asked if I had any more in the car, I said no. He then told me to get rid of the scissor, when I was about to toss it out of the car, he said to wait until he was gone because he did not want to give me a ticket for littering, too. Then he asked me what kind of work I did. I told him that I worked for the Illinois Department of Correction, Juvenile Division. He then gave me a short but firm lecture about working with kids and doing drugs. And since it was the weekend, he would let me go with just a warning for the scissor but a ticket for speeding. And if he ever caught me speeding in Missouri again, he would lock me up for as long as he could. I said, "Yes Sir," and thanked him for not taking me to jail for the scissor.

During the whole time we were going through my things, him seeing the scissor and lecturing me about doing drugs while working with kids, I kept thinking about where the bag of coke had landed. As he was getting out of the car I finally saw where, in the passenger seat! Somehow it ended up in the passenger seat and he had been sitting on it the entire time he was in my car! As he was getting out of the car the bag fell off the seat of his pants, leaving a white spot! I sat there transfixed, thinking about the incident that just had taken place and its consequences. Once I gathered my thoughts and drove off, I tossed the scissor out of the car but not the coke. I knew I had to get rid of it, too, just in case he realized, or someone informed him of the white power on the seat of his pants. After making sure no one was following or watching I consumed the remaining coke and drove the speed limit the rest of the way home! This was a milestone in my life and began the painfully slow restoration of my faith.

Life changes...

To share my difficulties related to my work at IYC, I befriended a coworker and teacher, Vicki, on my staffing unit. To my surprise, we started dating. We were an unlikely interracial couple. It was my first serious inter-racial relationship. Making it more difficult was the fact that her father took it particularly hard. This was unexpected because he was seen as a liberal in his business, but when it came to his daughter he distanced himself from us, which caused problems between her and her family. She then left IYC and started working in a retail store in a mall. I can't say for sure, but I think her father had something to do with it. While we were dating, I met some of her friends that also worked at the mall. One fall weekend day, I went to the mall to see Vicki and I noticed across from her store this buttermilk-skinned young lady working in a leather store. After visiting with Vicki, my curiosity about who this young lady was got the best of me and I had to meet her. So I went in to look at leather jackets, which was the furthest thing from my mind since I didn't like leather at all! I waited for her to come to help me so I could strike up a conversation, and once we talked I knew there was something special between us. I met Jean for the first time. A few weeks later, we all met at a party. The party was at Jean's and her best friend Lori's apartment. I knew that I and Vicki's relationship was on shaky ground, and when I found out that Jean was married, I was disappointed. We continued to hang out together as friends, and I found out that Jean's marriage was on very shaky grounds, as well; her husband wasn't living with her at that time. However, he did eventually move back in. We had very in-depth talks about our relationship and despite my strong feelings for Vicki, I found I had to tell Jean my strong feeling that we would someday be married!

In the meantime Vicki and I broke up due to problems within her family. I didn't want to be in a relationship that would cause problems because I knew how important a father figure was to a family since I didn't have one. Jean and her husband moved back to her hometown of Madison, Wisconsin, and I thought all hope was lost. Three years passed before Jean and I talked again. To my surprise her marriage had ended, and she called to let me know that "you can say I told you so" and she appreciated my friendship and support. As fate would have it, God had placed Jean in my life again and blessed us with a gorgeous and brilliant daughter, Joan Niccole "Nicci." Jean still had friends in Aurora and would occasionally come down for visits. This initiated the building of a close relationship, and it never turned back. To build on that fate, my Mom had moved to Madison years before to live with my sister. Due to deteriorating health reasons, she was in the loving care of my sister. My brother Sim and I would drive up to Madison almost every weekend for the next year or so to visit Mom. After our long-distance relationship, Jean had agreed to marry me and moved to Aurora the fall of 1988, just after she graduated college.

After working at the Department Of Corrections for eleven years, and my wife to be and our daughter had moved to Aurora, we started to plan our wedding. I thought the good life had finally happened for us. I was looking forward to leaving the single life behind and becoming a husband, a father and a parent. Some friends and coworkers made wagers that our marriage wasn't going to last. I had been a bachelor for a long time and was 41 when we got married and Jean was 30. It appeared that their prophecy would come true due to three delays in our wedding. The first delay was due to another serious knee injury, I tore my other patella tendon during our annual staff and student Christmas basketball game at IYC. We had to postpone our wedding and this led to me being forced into retirement from IYC. My wife to be, Jean, believed that our streak of misfortunes had something to do with her moving back to Aurora. They had only been there for a few months. She thought maybe we shouldn't get married; that she was **Bad Luck!** I insisted that the current events had nothing to do with her becoming my wife. Then the wedding was postponed for a second time after one of her bridesmaids, her sister Julie, became pregnant. The third setback was my forced resignation from IYC! Their reason for forcing me to resign was that they couldn't continue to employ anyone that was on long-term disability status. This time the knee injury was much more devastating than the one I suffered at Aurora College. Now I had a family to care for and the forced resignation affected my medical benefits, placing my family's well-being in jeopardy, especially my daughter, Nicci, who is asthmatic.

It all turned out to be a blessing in disguise because I needed a change from the daily ritual of an inhuman atmosphere — *not the clientele*, but some of the bureaucracy. So I took their forced resignation! We used my retirement package and an eventual settlement for my knee injury as a means of survival. This gave me some time to reevaluate my options, and I opted for a career in another type of counseling. That led me to a part-time counseling position at Open Door Clinic. Their primary vision was to provide sexual health and wellness educational services and treatment to those individuals who either had or were suspected of having a sexually transmitted disease (STD), including HIV and AIDS. This is when AIDS was still a mystery to most. Another blessing from God! The work I did at Open Door Clinic played a major role in shaping my intimacy outlook. It showed me the danger I had previously placed myself in by using drugs, watching adult entertainment and seeking out non-committed female companionship. This was God's way to me of reinforcing how dangerous intimacy was outside of marriage. For two years, I counseled women of all backgrounds and beauty levels, across all ethnic groups. They certainly didn't fit the stereotype that many would give to a STD clinic. Their treatment included all of the major STDs. This opened my eyes to the fact that these diseases did not discriminate; they did not care about whom they caught with their pants down, so to speak. It was an unbelievable sight to see so many men and women of prominent status, such as professionals, paraprofessionals, other practitioners and educators, come through that clinic. I realized I had been *playing Russian roulette* with my life from the lifestyle I had led. God was telling me as well as showing me that I needed to leave my vices behind, get married and settle down. Many of my clients had something in common, a prevalence of drugs and alcohol use which directly impacted their case.

Joys

Finally the Big day! On Saturday, October 21, 1989, Sweetest Day, Jean and I tied the knot or jumped the broom, as some would say. Basically, we were married in a small but lovely wedding ceremony of about seventy-five family members and close friends in Madison, Wisconsin. A casual reception followed that was joyful as we shared our love for one another. Everyone mingled and delighted in an array of delicious finger foods as tall tales were told, mostly about me (I think half the reason why my friends from Aurora came was because they were protecting their wagers and witnessing my historic end to bachelorhood). On Sunday, after the gift opening at my brother Jessie and his wife, Marie's, home in Madison, my wife and I left on our honeymoon, driving to Orlando, Florida. We wanted to take in the sights of Tennessee's Great Smoky Mountains and have some adult time together before enjoying Florida's attractions: Disney World, especially the Epcot Center, along with the remaining theme parks and Sea World. We planned to stay with Jean's brother, Rusty, and his wife, Nancy, in Orlando. The first leg of our trip took us to Lexington Kentucky, where we spent our second night together as husband and wife. It was a great night. The next morning we were up early, eager to reach Orlando but sleepiness forced us to spend the night in Ocoee, Florida. After we had checked into the hotel, my wife called her brother to inform them that we were staying the night in Ocoee so they wouldn't worry about us. We did not know about the events of the last couple days, since cell phones were not a part of the social network at that time.

Using the old reliable landline phone, my sister, by way of my now father-in-law, John Rustad, made contact with his son, Rusty, to inform me that Mom had ended her struggle with diabetes on October 24, 1989 at 4:45 p.m. Some say she hung on until I got married. I distinctly remember that conversation and how I felt afterward.

To say the least, we were very saddened to lose Mom, a kind-hearted woman and mother who eagerly gave her Agape Love and kindness to all without any misgivings. Her job was now complete! She taught us all what she knew about life's provision, stipulation and God's word. But I also must admit that I was relieved that God had ended her suffering and taken her home to be with Him and Jesus Christ. With Mom's death, our two-week honeymoon turned into a day of rest, a day touring the **Epcot Center** and a meal at a French restaurant in the **World Showcase**. Then Jean and I were back in the car for an eleven-plus hours trip to Louise, Mississippi, to attend Mom's farewell funeral celebration. We had to contact family members in Madison and Aurora to bring clothing for us to wear for Mom's funeral because the clothing we took on our honeymoon was not the proper attire for a Southern Baptist funeral. This was turning out to be quite a true adventure for us, especially for my wife, Jean. She had never been to Mississippi, let alone to my hometown of Louise or a highly emotional Baptist funeral. Jean was seeing all of this for the first time, my rural community of Anchor Curve, my hometown, Louise, my old school friends, our religious ceremony and eating our ethnic soul food all at once. As my friend Bernard Bridges would say, "she were the only fly in the buttermilk!" Having been in countless situations where I was the minority, I can imagine what it must have been like for her, being this buttermilk skinned Wisconsin woman at a highly emotional Baptist church service! We were surrounded by jam-packed church of African Americans that came to say their goodbyes to Madear. There was some uncontrollable crying and some passing out as the preachers continued to stir up more emotion. My sister and I were actually a bit upset about the theatrics because we did not want Mom's final goodbye to become one filled with emotion, since Mom always taught us to live life by faith not by our sight or emotions.

After the church service and burial, everyone gathered at Aunt Pearlie and Uncle Joe Willie's house for a feast that was prepared by some of the greatest soul food cooks in our surrounding community. They made macaroni and cheese; collard greens and cornbread; southern fried chicken, okra, sweet potatoes, apple pies, pecan pies and peach cobblers. German chocolate, coconut and caramel cakes were also a part of that great feast. Following the feast into that evening and night was another ritual, storytelling. Of course, most of their stories were aimed directly at me to poke fun of me in front of my new wife, and oh, how they could tell them! Some of their tall tales were harmless; for instance, how I fell asleep with that goat bone in my jaw all night and earned the nickname Goat Jones. But others played a more significant role in my life when I mistakenly drank the Clorox or how much I cried when Dr. Macklin gave me a shot with a needle so dull he had to force it into my arm with both hands. That shot would later cause me to see visions of heat monkeys that weren't coming from a hot highway. And let's not forget about me having the chickenpox so bad that I had to wear one of my sister's dresses for two weeks! Finally, I was reminded of my clumsiness in the Wile E. Coyote fall! As time passed into the night I tried to keep busy and not think of the great loss we had all suffered. As the week of preparation for Mom's funeral and burial ceremony had come to an end, there was a tremendous outpouring of love, support and outstanding feasts to consummate the exceptional life of Lizzie Josephine Fountain, *Madear!* Now as everyone started to prepare for their journey home, it came to me that Mom was already at home with God and Christ!

Under the circumstances of Mom's death, Jean and I still had an exceptional but shortened honeymoon. I had spent the first twenty years of my life in Mississippi, with an occasional trip to New Orleans. But this time, the trip from Orlando, Florida, to Louise, Mississippi, up Interstate 10 by way of Pensacola, Florida, along the coast was very fascinating for two reasons. I was seeing white sandy beaches, especially around Pensacola, Florida, for the first time and this was the vacationing spot of the family that Mom use to babysit for, the Stoners, and on many occasions they took her vacationing with them to watch their two children, Steven and Mae Francis. The consummation of the total trip was seeing the expression on my wife's face that said "she got it." She understood all the things I had tried to explain to her about Mississippi; how I had grown up in contemporary slavery and the inhumanity of the 1950s and 60s.

Once back home in Aurora, I resumed my counseling responsibilities with the Open Clinic clients. Shortly thereafter, my wife informed me she was pregnant, surprise, surprise! And the money from my retirement and settlement was gone. Although Jean was working, I still felt I had to find a second job to secure more income. So I thought to myself, "where can I get that second job to earn extra money that wouldn't have me working long hours and weekends leaving no time for family and sports?" Of course, there were no jobs to be found. And the pressure of not being able to secure that second job was taking a toll on me. My adversary continued to try and block our blessings from God, using Mom's death and having a baby on the way to put more pressure on me. Now I was even more deeply involved in illegal activities. The money coming in was great; however, the risk and life-style was one of devastation. I had to closely watch each step I made; I didn't go home the same way all the time. I was suspicious of everyone, outside of my immediate family, who might rob me, rat me out to the police or harm Jean or Nicci, especially those who couldn't pay for their fix each time they needed one. More importantly, I had to be aware of those whom I purchased my product from because there is no honor among the unrighteous. As it turned out, my suspicions did have merit. Jean had gone to Madison for the weekend and taken Nicci with her to assist her sister Joan in preparing for a performance by the band, Cheap Trick. Joan was their road manager. At the end of the work day on Friday, I came home to plan out my weekend. A friend Monica stopped by the house and asked if I wanted to go to the Fox Valley Mall with her to eat at Red Lobster. Happily, I said yes because Red Lobster was one of my favorite restaurants, and we were off to the mall.

Because it was a Friday, the mall was jammed with people and my suspicions began to rise as to why Monica asked me out to Red Lobster since Jean and I always took our daughter Nicci there to eat. The next question was, did she know Jean and I took Nicci there regularly? Was it for someone to see us there together and go back and tell Jean? If that was the reason, it didn't have merit because Jean and I shared everything and I would tell her myself.

Once inside Red Lobster, it seemed to take her a very long time to place her order and once the food did arrive, she followed the same process to eat, taking a very long time. Followed by her wanting to just walk around the mall, this made me very uneasy as to what kind of set up this was. Was she trying to break up my marriage, or what was the reason behind this display? I was being suspicious for the wrong reason; it had nothing to do directly with Jean and me, as I found out later that evening. When we drove up to the house, she was in such a hurry to leave and I still hadn't figured it out until after I opened the garage door and was inside. Then a light went on inside my stupid head as I could feel the warm heat coming through the door that led to the kitchen from the garage. As I approached the door that led into the kitchen, I could see the kitchen window was open. I knew then that someone had broken into the house, but I was not quite sure who was behind it. I knew I had hid my stash where no one could find it. So my next step was to call the police in case they were still hiding somewhere in our two-bedroom ranch house. After the police arrived, and I went to take an inventory of what was missing, that's when I knew who was behind that break-in. They had taken the television out of the master bedroom and placed it in the living room. A pillowcase off our bed was used to put my expense vintage wine in that I had brought from Germany. They also took Jean's jewelry including her wedding band and some of her grandmother's heirloom jewelry. They didn't take any of my personal items, e.g., my new Air Jordans, and expensive suits, dress shoes or jewelry.

The police thought they must have been in the house when I came home because the television set from our bedroom was in the family room with its cord wrapped around it and the corner was damaged. However, they were able to take the VCR from the living room along with the other items mentioned. After the police had gone, I went to check on my stash and it was still there. I then called a couple of the guys to see where they were during the break-in and their whereabouts ruled them out. A couple hours later, the guy I once considered a close friend and did all my weekend business with came by to let me know he had been in back of my house by the window where the thieves entered. He said he was looking for me after he had tried the front door and he knew Jean was gone. He didn't want me to think he was the one who had broken into my house, since my neighbors might have seen him in the back yard; he also wanted to know if I needed anything or if they got my stash. If they got my stash, he would replace it for free. I told him I did not keep it in the house (although I did) and I was okay. I was sorry that my wife's jewelry and family heirlooms had been taken. I never told him or Monica that I believed they were in on the break-in of our home and how much hurt Jean felt by that violation and invading her personal things as they ransacked our home.

Afterwards, I had a couple close calls with an undercover police officer following me in his car with the headlights turned off for blocks, possibly hoping that I would lead him or them to my stash or other individuals who used or sold those illegal drugs for a bust. He followed me to the house, and I immediately flushed my stash down the toilet. I knew it was time for me to get out of Aurora. God was warning me again to get away from my newly formed illegal assemblage and let Him find me a job to take care of me and my family so I wouldn't end up in jail or a correctional facility like the ones I once sent juvenile offenders to. A week later, on one of those late Saturday nights when I was normally out conducting business I decided to stay home. I was sitting outside on the new patio that my father-in-law had helped me build that summer. A voice came to me out of nowhere and said "move to Madison" and when I turned around to see who was telling me to move, there was no one there. So I immediately got up and went inside the house to see if it was Jean playing tricks with my mind knowing that I was most likely stoned. Once inside the house I could tell that she hadn't moved from where she was sitting when I went outside. She knew that something was wrong by the look on my face and how I was looking at her. So she asked me what was wrong. Without hesitating, I asked her how long would it take for her to get ready to move to Madison after our child was born? We had chosen not to know the sex of our baby. Looking at me strangely but surprisingly she said two weeks. For some strange reason, I knew this was the last chance for me to leave Aurora on my own before facing some great embarrassment or possible incarceration. Jean was eight months pregnant and we just had celebrated our first wedding anniversary, and here I was again involved with drugs. This time, I was placing not only my life in jeopardy but my family.

The following Monday morning I called my attorney. He was a former teammate and classmate who had completed the paperwork some five years ago to help me purchase the house, as a fixer upper, for around $40,000. I desperately needed to sell it, and I was hoping to make a profit for a new start in Madison. I had put so much hard work and money into fixing it up. My attorney helped me to find a realtor and completed the paperwork to place the house on the market; within a week, a former co-worker and friend made me an offer of $75,000 dollars for the house. I sold the house to him under the condition that we could rent the house from him for one month, giving Jean enough time to recover after Marshall's birth before moving to Madison, Christmas 1990.

After making the move to Madison, I began to lose contact with my friends, and the brotherhood that I thought we had formed started to unravel. Even after all the adventures we lived and shared, they now began to be swept away by distance. Even my best man in my wedding, Leo, lost contact with us after he stopped returning my phone calls. I then started to question myself as to were these guys true friends or were they like all those other con artists but with a different agenda or purpose! All of this began to take a toll on me, to the point I started to question myself. What kind of person was I? And what type individuals had I befriended and why did I not see this coming? It became very apparent that they were in this make-believe friendship only for the advancement of their own personal benefit and nothing else mattered. Even after I had put my life on the line on many occasion to support their enterprises, I thought that they would have done the same thing for me. Apparently, I was wrong to think that way or put my trust in them. Even if I had done something to offend them, especially my best man, and we were friends for such a long period of time, he would have at least let me know what had happened between us, if anything, to cause his reluctance to stay in contact. He should have been man enough to confront me to work it out for our friendship's sake.

The only one to stay in contact with me all through the years was Bernard. The very one that I thought would be the first one to sever ties with me. Not that I thought he was less a friend than the others; it was just that Bridges, as I called him, is the type of person who lets you know that he did things to benefit him. He was straight up and for that reason I should have known he was a true friend and he did not camouflage his intention of being a friend like the others. For example, Bridges knew how to play the game of tennis very well and knew I didn't have a clue; he never told me or showed me any instruction on how to grip the racquet or hit the ball. He would just take me out and demoralize me on the tennis court and take me back home. So the only way I could retaliate was on the basketball court at work, where I had the huge advantage and a chance for payback! Isn't it funny some of the things we choose to remember and not to remember? How things turned out in my life is different than what I expected.

Chapter 19

TRUE ENLIGHTENMENT

With a mustard seed of faith I could at least believe I was **this**, a child of God. With constant doses of His Word and a growing helper in my heart, He taught me to believe in Him enough to at least start making decisions like I was a child of God. All the while I was preoccupied with **this** and **that**, Romans 1:5 was hard at work. My obedience flowed directly from my faith to believe I was who God said I was, even when I acted like **that** instead of **this**, the more I felt blessed, chosen, adopted, favored, redeemed and forgiven. I believe that anyone can know and comply with the fruit of obedience. If I can know and live victoriously through the power of the Holy Spirit, anyone can.

1 Corinthian 1-3. Paul described what a carnal Christian's faith was and how true spiritual faithfulness is grown.

Let me step back from my narrative and give you my thoughts. I had not yet known or experienced this faithfulness. Paul attributes this setback to the lack of spiritual development that hindered my faithfulness. I had not applied what I had already learned to receive advanced training (solid food) in biblical knowledge. My most notable example that set the tone was as a young adult fresh out of high school. I was unaware of Paul's description of a carnal Christian, placing me in a spiritual infancy of being fed on God's word. As I had described, my main focus had become worldly fame or self-centeredness more than my Christian belief and faith after losing that high school basketball championship game. Subconsciously, was I still blaming God for that loss? At that time, I was unaware that my self-centered lifestyle was one of a carnal Christian for more than two decades to come after high school. Therefore, by not applying what I learned at an early age and through high school, day by day God's word, my protective shield became weak, opening doors in my life for worldly things that I once was shielded from by my spiritual intellects. Once the door to this world system deception was open, before I realized it I was caught up in a whirlwind of self-centeredness and doubts that seemed endless. I continued to hide my early Christian upbringing of faithfulness and loyalty to Christ instilled in me from Mom and Grandma Retta's biblical teaching. I cowardly failed to acknowledge my Christian faith and witness for Christ. Doing so, I deliberately concealed my personal testimony, fearing what my immoral subculture social groupies might think of me. I was unable to grow spiritually.

The most important lesson I learned through my various ordeals was when there is an elapse in my spiritual growth, *doubts and falsehood* grow rapidly. I needed to get back in touch with the Holy Spirit inside of me by acknowledging that I loved the Lord my God and Savior with all my heart and soul, more than anything. I needed to start reading the Bible daily, allowing its teachings to stir my heart and spirit, as well as to fill my spiritual intellect and apply that understanding daily to my life. In the book James 1:6-8 it explains, *"But let him ask in faith, with no doubting, for he who doubts is like a wave of the sea driven and tossed by the wind. For let not that man suppose that he will receive anything from the Lord; he is a double minded man unable in all his ways."* I had let doubts become a part of my life and they tossed my emotions like I was on a rollercoaster rising into life's infinity. My emotions were being tossed into a deeper sense of false hope that I could still receive the Lord's blessings as a carnal Christian. So I had to take a step back and look closer at *doubts* and their origins.

What I had failed to realize was that the first doubt spoken or recorded came from Satan—surprise, surprise—as a serpent's mouth as in Genesis, Chapter 3. I, too, had let uncertainties and misgivings be used as a weapon to defeat me by driving a wedge between me and my God. For me, this defeatist way of life revealed itself in many different methods of deception that I let lure me, a once faithful servant, into believing there is a God but not believing *IN* God or trusting in His word. Doubts hindered my walk within God's righteousness, stopping the two most important things I needed in life to survive: God's salvation and Grace, since my righteousness without faith is no more than filthy rags to God, *Isaiah 64:6*. For more than three decades these uncertainties became contagious, causing me to drop my shield of faith to life's immoral vulnerabilities. I had let myself become that *city without walls and broken down, Proverbs 25:28*, as life's worries filled my heart and mind, with doubts that had me believing that since I was born with learning disabilities and dirt poor in Mississippi, I was born to be a failure.

I am not saying these verses represent you in any way personally, but they can help anyone understand who God's word says they are in His sight.

Chapter 20

WAUSAU BY THE WAY OF MADISON!

Ephesians 4:30: "Do not grieve the Holy Spirit of God, by who you are sealed for the day of redemption."

Wausau, a city I once called Home by the way of a city in serious transition, Madison, Wisconsin, 1991. At that time, Madison was a city in serious transition and so was I. God had now blessed us with two wonderful children, Nicci and Marsh. My wife was very happy because she was back at home in Madison with family and friends. And I was happy for her. I, too, had family in Madison, and that made it a homecoming for both of us. After paying the Aurora taxes, closing costs and our other bills we took just enough money out of escrow earnings with us for Christmas and to live off until we could secure employment. The goal was to purchase another house. I left the remaining money from our escrow behind in our credit union in Aurora.

The job market in Madison wasn't what I expected or pictured it to be for someone like myself, with a bachelor degree in Criminal Justice and eleven years of experience working in juvenile counseling for the department of corrections. Employers with openings in the field of counseling wanted candidates who had a master's degree and or a certificate of certification within the state of Wisconsin. I was not their ideal candidate even with all those years of experience. With our money continuing to decrease, I needed desperately to do something to replenish our dwindling funds. Therefore, in order for me to become employable I needed to return to school. The spring semester of 1992, I enrolled at the University of Wisconsin Madison to complete a master's degree in the field of Criminal Justice with strong emphasis on social work that I had initiated at Aurora College while working for the Open Door Clinic. A couple weeks into classes when I went to pay my tuition and buy books, I wrote a check on our account at the credit union in Aurora for five hundred dollars. The check came back marked insufficient funds. I was perplexed with that turn of events because I had left a considerable amount of money in the Aurora credit union. So the University was very nice and they gave me two weeks to clear up what I thought was a misunderstanding by the credit union. So I called the credit union inquiring about insufficient funds status on our account and what I needed to do in order to get things cleared up. They informed me the Internal Revenue Service, IRS, had frozen our accounts. I then proceeded to contact the IRS for the reasons why they had frozen our accounts with the credit union. They informed I had too many possessions in my name: three cars, a house and I had just deposited over forty thousand dollars. They felt it didn't match the income I earned from working with the department of corrections. The only thing on their list I couldn't justify was one of the cars in my name. In order to avoid a hearing and possible other embarrassment I opted for the penalty, not knowing that the fine was going to cost us the remaining money from our account. The IRS would eventually charge us twenty-one percent interest on each dollar they took. Since I couldn't reinvest what they had taken, it took us several years to finally pay them off.

Near destitution in Madison

Now here we were in Madison with only a few thousand dollars remaining from the money we took for Christmas and to live off until we could secure employment. I had to drop out of school and start looking for any job I could find. With some assistance from a cousin, Cora White, I was able to land a job as a drug counselor, how ironic, for a detoxification unit. They provided a wide array of human services; addressing problems relating to alcohol, substance abuse and addictions; mental illness, and homelessness. After working for Tellurian for about a year in their detoxification unit, the owner and president, Mr. Michael Florek, had to make some cutbacks in staff that was going to leave me out of a job. Fortunately for me, the program's accounting department also handled the bookkeeping for an after-school educational and tutoring program named Project Bootstrap Audio

Visual Production, Incorporated. Bootstrap was looking for a program director, and I was recommended. I would become the Program Director for Bootstrap, earning just enough to make ends meet, and worked there for four years. Bootstrap counseled, mentored and gave academic tutorial assistance to at-risk, latch key and nontraditional middle and high school students of the Madison Area School District. I also assisted a psychologist with the required group counseling for participants' acceptance into the Bootstrap program. We had worked together for three years and Bootstrap had made significant progress and growth, even passing a required external audit. As with any program, with growth comes change and down-sizing, and Bootstrap was about to experience both. So there needed to be a change made in the administration, and I knew that it was going to be me. I just didn't know how it all was going to play itself out.

The psychologist for Bootstrap witnessed my skills firsthand in how well I worked with and was able to relate to troubled adolescents. He invited me to speak at a residential group home for girls a few miles south-east of Madison, which was under the umbrella of a traditional adolescent residential program in rural North Central Wisconsin. Shortly after that speaking engagement, things started to go south with my employment at Bootstrap, as I had expected it to. I had delivered a stern speech on truancy at a symposium called "Madison: A City in Transition Call to Action" that didn't sit well with some of the elite community leaders. I knew my time in Madison and at Bootstrap was limited. The psychologist contacted me and told me he knew of a job that had my name written all over it, but it was at a traditional youth residential program in rural North Central Wisconsin. My reluctance to go to rural Wisconsin soon changed after I learned that my services were no longer a priority at Bootstrap. I understood that since Bootstrap's main funding source came from Dane County and the City of Madison that it wasn't fruitful to speak poorly of them. So for the best interest of all, I bowed out and applied for the job as Multicultural Director at that traditional adolescent residential program, Home Youth and Family Programs in Wittenberg.

In the end, Madison was the most important step in my life in so many ways. While living there, I had access to a strong Christian faith in my sister, Lueretha. My father-in-law, John, gave me the educational support I needed so desperately, which had evaded me thus far. With the help of my father-in-law, I began to really understand the power of a good education. My sister helped me to understand and return to my *Faith* in God and Christ.

In mid–July 1996, I accepted the position of Multicultural Director despite some misgivings as to what might lie ahead. This traditional adolescent residential program was one without walls topped with razor wire, like IYC, located in a rural town. Jean and I visited the program and thought it offered a good opportunity for me to utilize my skills and experience in counseling and mentoring at-risk, nontraditional, latch key and delinquent adolescents. Living in this rural town would have been more convenient, but we decided that Wausau would be a better place to live. Among many other positive attributes, we chose Wausau, moving there in August 1996, because of the good schools, the fact that it was the largest city in North Central Wisconsin and we assumed we would fit in better, as well as the beauty and vibrancy of the city. But there were a few other underlying factors, as well. I've had some unpleasant experiences in small, rural communities. My observations are that some individuals who choose that lifestyle aren't exactly the type of people you'd see in a Norman Rockwell painting. If these individuals had their way, they'd replace the town's Welcome signs with Keep Out signs! And if you're an interracial couple, you'd better not even ask for directions out of town. It is ridiculous to think that the majority of small town folks fit into this stereotype. It's probably very few, but I've learned to be wary or err on the side of caution.

Unfortunately, this type of belligerent you-don't-belong-here attitude eventually began to surface at my new workplace. The administration did their best to police the situation, but it nonetheless continued. It seemed as though some people just weren't ready to accept minorities in a supervisory role, let alone make changes. After three years plus of commuting forty-five minutes one way each day from Wausau, which turned into an hour's commute with hazardous road conditions in the winter months, and facing what seemed to be an ongoing undercurrent of workplace harassment, a decision was inevitable! From derogatory statements written, signed and left underneath my office door by support staff in protest of changes I had made, to me being accused of being the harasser instead of being the harassed, it was time to make a decision: should I stay or go?

One day, after praying and talking with one of the program's therapists and one of the teachers, they assured me that God could use my talents anywhere, as long as

I was working toward the betterment of His Kingdom. Therefore, I resigned in October 1999 and relied on my faith in God and Christ to find other work where I could help young people.

I finally landed a part-time job as an elementary school teacher's aide for the Wausau Area School District, WASD. In this role, I saw the need for an after-school program similar to Bootstraps. My son, Marsh, also spoke of his friends at a different elementary school who needed help with their studies. Since I was an at-risk and nontraditional student, I felt compelled to help in some way. A follow-up assessment showed there were no after-school educational, tutoring, mentoring and bilingual support programs within the WASD to assist those at-risk and nontraditional students and their parents. The WASD demographics continued to change, caused in part by families migrating to Wausau for a better life, to escape the socioeconomic problems they were facing in places like Central America, Asia and our large metropolitan inner cities, e.g., Chicago and Milwaukee. There was an increased burden on the educational, social and judicial institutions. The public elementary schools in particular were experiencing some difficulty with the increasing numbers and complexities of assisting adolescents and their families who had problems making a positive transition from their previous educational systems.

From the data I collected and with my then twenty-five-plus years of experience in working with at-risk, latch key and nontraditional adolescents from various venues and programs, I began to work on developing an after-school mentoring, educational and tutoring concept that my wife, daughter, son, and I eventually named

Family Advocacy Mentoring, Inc. and called it FAM. Not knowing at the time that I was developing and implementing a concept of mentoring into FAM that included one of the oldest methods of teaching adolescents. Its first recorded modern usage of the term can be traced to a book entitled "Les Adventures de Telemaque", by the French writer, François Fénelon. From this book, I learned that the lead character is that of a Mentor. The book was published in 1699 and was very popular during the 18th century, and the modern applications of the term can be traced to that publication. This is the source of the modern use of the word: Mentor–a trusted friend, counselor or teacher, usually a more experienced person.

Before reading the origin of being a mentor, I initially thought that FAM's mentoring concept would be a cinch. I had more than twenty-five years of experience in counseling and mentoring youthful offenders from juvenile corrections to residential treatment programs. What I failed to realize was that my then clientele was from a controlled environment, and managing their behavior was much different from a non-controlled environment. For instance, the youthful offenders had a stricter protocol to adhere to than those adolescents in communities and school programs. With hindsight, this became more prevalent to me because when a youthful offender was paroled they lost much of that strict protocol, which usually caused them to violate parole status within weeks of being paroled.

As FAM's Executive Director and Director of Mentoring, I had to incorporate a system of protocol that would hold each participant accountable for his or her behavior in the community as it did in school and FAM.

Therefore, with assistance from board members, I was able to redesign FAM's infrastructure and mission statement to involve a daily accountability that focused on creating a moral compass to provide many opportunities for positive development in our schools, communities and society.

I built FAM's legacy with the help of many others on those concepts and HOPE that began in 2000 with two participants, Jose and Bryce, with a philosophy that it is never too late, or too early, to provide any adolescent and their parents with positive, life-shaping influences. FAM was implemented. Making FAM the WASD's first and only after-school, private, nonprofit organization to track its elementary participants' progress through middle school into high school. Through FAM's life-shaping influences and a plan of action, I made sure each participant received that early educational foundation that I never had, dedicated to improving communication between students and school, family and community.

My vision for FAM was also built on my upbringing and family values that it took a whole village (community) to raise one adolescent. By taking a fellowship approach to educating not only the participants but parents, guardians, family and/or other community members involved in a hopeful, healthy, safe and diverse support community environment, FAM's village, or community, philosophy was also built on the fact that each successful adult often cited a childhood mentor *aside from parents* as the one person who most profoundly influenced their lives and instilled HOPE!

More and more, I have been convinced that the perseverance and diligence that I learned as a child of a sharecropper in the 50s, are qualities that some students today need more and more of in this competitive society. My belief in faith in the Lord Jesus Christ helped me to endure hard times and prejudices that were so commonplace at that time. It taught me to be thankful, to have a forgiving heart, and to use the *equipment* that God has blessed me with, and not blame others.

Dr. George Washington Carver once said, "You've all the tools the greatest men have had, two arms, two hands, two legs, two eyes and a brain to use if you would be wise. With this *equipment* they all began, so start for the top and say '*I can*.' Look them over, the wise and the great, they take their food from a common plate... Similar knives and forks they use, with similar laces they tie their shoes... You are the handicap you must face. By knowing that courage, hope and faith must come from within, for each of us must furnish the will to win. So figure it out for yourself, my child, you were born with all that the great have had. With your *equipment* they all began, get a hold of yourself and say: '*I can*.'"

Chapter 21

A TRAGEDY HITS HOME...

Psalm 31:1 "In You, O Lord, I put my trust"

On December 4, 2002, months short of FAM's second year anniversary, an organization I had built on HOPE through faith in GOD and Christ, a tragedy on that day profoundly shook my faith when it struck my family, instead of a participant's family. A faith that had been steadfast in our family history since our enslaved ancestors passed down through Mom and Grandma Retta.

Through my zigzag journey, from life as a dirt-poor southern black child as "Hey, Water Boy" and a two cap pistol-gun wearing cowboy preadolescent; to those dreadful Wednesday corporal punishment days filled with embarrassment; to life on the tough streets of Chicago; to the radical days of *make love, not war* drug-filled streets of Oakland; to Coahoma Junior College – Coach Gain's stogie cigar and nineteen-fifty-nine long-distance run; to the second encounter of the appalling streets of Chicago; to the impeccable cosmetic campus of Aurora College;

to Madison, a city in a serious ethnicity transition; to Wausau, the whitest congressional district in the United States in the 80s, the city my family and I had once called home, I have experienced both the evils of poverty and prejudice. Complicated with adversities; a victim of con artists turned predator; surrendered and succumbed to drugs, adult entertainment and alcohol abuse; integrity and values fall to hypocrisy, had once encompassed my life. Not any of that had prepared me for that phone call I received on that Wednesday morning (9:00 o'clock a.m.).

The Call!

That phone call tested my faith to its breaking point, and it took a book almost a decade later, THE SHACK, which would help in explaining it all! Explaining why I needed to surrender my earthly *independence* of free will back to God and Christ! From that book, I learned a vital lesson about controlling my *free will* and how it only allows me to be in one place at a time. Therefore, how could I protect the ones I love so dearly that lived miles away when I couldn't even protect my wife and children when they were out of my sight? Unaware that holding on to my *free will* had always placed me in a vulnerable situation when it came to the protection of my loved ones. Earlier, I had made reference to the way I once lived my life without God and Christ. It was like playing *Russian Roulette*. However, there is another dangerous game of chance that I was still playing, on a regular basis, with my and my family's life. Who would I blame for a profound tragedy? Do I blame myself? Or do I blame God and Christ for not stepping in and stopping that tragedy?

As a mortal human being, I let my own self-independence *of free will* set the courses and ground rules in this game. I needed a spiritual protector, especially when raising children, in a country whose system over time often stems from some type of greed that leads to violence. Christ through God the Father and their Helper (the Holy Spirit) is that protecting force.

I was like the *BALL* of the *Roulette Wheel that spins and launches out of control*, not knowing where it is going to land. I was leaving my life destiny to chance without God's will in control of it. I was spinning around in a danger zone not knowing when my number in life would be called. As I was being twisted and turned in life, as G-force training twists and turns its jet pilots, causing me to lose all hope, faith and love, with love being the most important one. Finally, I was spun into a state of depression and desperation that told me you can't even think of tomorrow because I don't even know how on earth I was going to get or live through today.

These were the feelings I had after receiving that alarming morning phone call on Wednesday December 4, 2002, from my sister in Madison. She informed me that our brother Jesse's second oldest, my nineteen-year-old niece Lizzette (about one year older than my daughter Nicci) had been found dead in her Fitchburg, Wisconsin, apartment. The Fitchburg police department was calling her death suspicious. It was all over the news stations, and they needed me there with the family. I immediately called my wife at work and informed her of this shocking news and proceeded to call FAM's staff and the WASD personnel to let them know that I would be closing FAM for an undetermined amount of time due to a family emergency. The next step, I thought, was the most difficult one, telling my nineteen-year-old daughter that her cousin and friend was dead and explaining it to Marsh, my twelve-year-old son. Shaken from the news of Lizzette, I let my immediate focus turn toward my family.

The drive to Madison

To say the least, I was filled with anxiety about how I was going to help my family in their time of need. I had helped so many families over my twenty-five-plus years of counseling and mentoring them in their time of need from some kind of tragedy or just every day survival. This time it was different and would be more difficult to tell family members how to fill that now empty void of losing a loved one and not to retaliate but let law enforcement and the court system handle it. What was the lesson or message to be learned from this tragedy? Was it a way to test my counseling skills, faith or bring us closer together and to God and Christ? And of course, there was that question and blame that everyone seems to ask in a time like that, "Why?" Why did God let it happen, or why did it have to happen to a person who had so much going for herself?

My wife and our son must have been filled with anxiety about what they were going to say and do once we reached Madison, because there was not much conversation being carried on during the entire two-and-a-half-hour trip. Except for an occasional question aimed toward me, asking if I was okay. Or how was our daughter, Nicci, doing driving to Madison by herself from college at the University of Wisconsin Green Bay? The trip seemed long yet short, depending on what state of mind I was in: wanting to know more about what had happened and concerned about Nicci. But when it came down to what I could say or do to help ease their pains, it made the trip seem shorter. Once we finally arrived at my brother's house, there were other family members and friends standing outside in front of the house. Many of them had spent several hours at the Fitchburg police station, and there were discussions on the vague information they had learned about the possible cause of Lizzette's death. Opinions were forming as to what had happened and what should be done about it if justice was not served. I, Jean and our son, Marsh, said our hellos to the outside assemblage, and we proceeded into the house to see my brother Jesse, his wife, Marie, their daughter Jessica and son JoJo. Once inside their home I could see and feel the devastating grip that this evil act had on them. Their home atmosphere was filled with *excruciating pain of disbelief and heartache*, and the age old question "WHY?" That question that has plagued mankind since the Garden of Eden was displayed on the faces of the entire assembly, including my family and me. My brother was sitting in his easy chair with a book in his hand titled, *"What to do when the Police are gone."* His wife Marie was sitting in her favorite chair in a paralyzed state of mind, as if her soul had been shaken to the core of disbelief. I walked over to my brother and placed my hand on his shoulder, as I said to him, "you don't need to read this book." I was there to help in any way I could, but he should place all of his pains and sorrows in the Lord's trusting hands. And I told him that we all needed *God and Christ* our savior more now than ever. THEY were there with us all; all we had to do was to let THEM in.

Throughout that evening and into the night, I could see the nature of evil trying so desperately to cast an even deeper devastation over our entire family by trying to ignite our natural inclination into retaliation for the death of our beloved Lizzette, a daughter, sister, niece, aunt, cousin, friend, artist and caretaker. While we were waiting for the coroner to come and bring the result of his autopsy, we prayed and tried to hold our family together. I gave thanks to God that our spiritual nature prevailed over our natural one that night and throughout the trial. The Chief Medical Examiner finally came around 8:30 P.M. or so that night and his report stated that it was a criminal investigation and he could not release the cause of death, but it was a traumatic death without any doubt! Even though we all were devastated with Lizzette's death, her mother, Marie, was overwhelmed the most. Those words "traumatic death" hit us, especially Marie, like a double-edged sword cutting into the already devastating wound behind Lizzette's death. Over the next month or so, the investigation into her death began to show some progress into naming a suspect or suspects. In the meantime, Lizzette's body had been released to the family to be prepared for a farewell celebration. We all, at one time or another, had gathered to celebrate holidays, childbirth, birthdays and graduations: family, friends, classmates, coworkers and others to celebrate, share stories, accomplishments and rejoice in the wonderful memory of our beloved Lizzette, as we said our final earthly mortal goodbyes to her on a wintry sunny Sunday, December 15, 2002.

The first part of closure came soon after her death, which was the cleaning of her apartment after the investigation was over and all the forensic evidence had been collected. It was very hard to see the food she had prepared for supper that evening was still on the stove and her well-groomed apartment was torn apart by the police investigation. Saying our earthly goodbyes to Lizzette at a loving and heartfelt service I initially thought was the most overwhelming event since Mom's death, but it wasn't any comparison to what was revealed at the murder trial.

While still waiting for Lizzette's murder trial to begin, which actually took almost three years, I attempted to return to my normal everyday operation of FAM, trying to hold my family together as I tried to give support to my brother and his family from afar and continue to serve God daily.

June of 2003, Lizzette's boyfriend was charged and arraigned for her murder. This was a relief and the beginning of a closure that someone had been charged with taking Lizzette's life. She was shot at close range one time. I didn't realize when a tragedy strikes home just how deeply it would impact me and my entire family. When I counseled or mentored other clients who had to deal with a tragedy I didn't experience the total impact of it. Her death left me in a hopeless state of mind for some time, with many sleepless nights. I had to seek counseling for myself from my personal physician, Dr. Steven Nichols, and medication to aide me in being able to sleep at night. With his counseling and prescribing something as simple as Tylenol PM, I let God do the rest. I was able to function well enough to keep my emotions under control, so I would be strong for my family, extended family and my FAM family. In the midst of all of this family stress and the stress of FAM possibly closing its doors, God sent us a savior!

A God Sent Man

FAM was in desperate need of a savior. We had made plans to close our doors in May of 2004 due to lack of funds. Through a good friend, Kathy Johnson, I was invited to speak at a networking event sponsored by the Rotary Club in Wausau. I met Patrick Bradley, a financial advisor who Kathy worked for, and after the speech about FAM, he said he had someone he would like me to meet. He said there was potential that he knew someone who could help financially in sustaining FAM that year.

What an incredible blessing it was that I then met this generous mystery entrepreneur, Mr. Robert Weirauch. I knew he was a good man because he came to my humble office instead of his professional office. Patrick and I were waiting for Mr. Weirauch and I happened to notice a casual-looking gentlemen walking past my basement office's window and to my surprise Patrick said, "There's Bob!" As you might imagine, I was expecting a business-attired meeting, and seeing the casualness of Bob was very refreshing. From our first meeting, he made me feel important and accepted as a peer. I was prepared for the meeting with all my data and statistics from the beginning of FAM, and he sat at the table and we struck up a casual conversation. A lifetime friendship was built. We never looked at the data I was ready to present. He wanted to know if what he had heard about me and the program were true, and he wasn't interested in statistics. Before Bob left that day, he made sure that FAM was financially secure for the remainder of that school year. And that was just the beginning of his generosity and devotion to FAM and my family! Meeting Bob changed the course of my life and reinforced that God has angels here on earth. He was a truly God-sent savior because he saved me, my family and my FAM family for years.

Still waiting for a trial

Two and a half years had passed and we were still waiting for closure via a trial to begin for Lizzette's murder. Now it was early April 2005, and I was back at Dr. Nichols' office. This time, I was seeking medication and information for release from an on-and-off nagging back pain. As fate would have it, once again my faith would be put to the test as another possible tragedy tried so desperately to enter into my immediate family with life-threatening complications. I began to ask God WHY I was now facing another possible life-threatening disaster, especially since I hadn't finished mourning or putting closure to Lizzette's death with a trial.

Usually during early spring. I am outside working in my garden, clearing up all the left-over fall foliage; removing old seasonal plants; threshing the dead foliage off the lawn and preparing the garden soil for new seedlings. The refurbishing always gave our garden a new natural look and balance of a beautiful and relaxing atmosphere that I so deeply needed in my life at that time. Working in my garden always gave me a peace of mind, and as those beautiful mixtures of perennials started to recover from the harshness of winter, so did I start to recover from Lizzette's death. As the landscaping progressed, I used decorative masonry bricks to outline the additional space to plant my new seedlings annuals to add a mixture to the perennials. About midway into the implementation of the new developed landscaping, I felt this agonizing pain in my lower back. Wanting to complete the task at hand, I attempted to ignore the elevated pain. The more I tried to ignore this unbearable pain the more severe it became to the point I had to retire to the defeat of bricks, when I had easily handled retaining wall blocks effortlessly. With much regret, I had no option but to surrender to the pain, retire to the couch and called Dr. Nichols. Knowing my back medical history, Dr. Nichols usually would have told me to take some extra strength pain reliever and relax for a few days. But this time he insisted that I come to his office to see him.

The appointment!

The next day, I went see Dr. Nichols to have a physical examination of my lower back, and an x-ray showed no major damage to the lower back vertebrae. A follow-up appointment was made for me to have an ultrasound procedure done. A week later, I went back to see Dr. Nichols to get the results from the ultrasound that had revealed the same diagnosis as the x-ray: no viewable damage to the vertebrates. Therefore my working with the masonry bricks to build that new extension for the new seedling bed wasn't the cause of my back pain. So the next question was what was causing the lower back pain that the x-ray and an ultrasound could not detect? The next step was to take a more in-depth look with an MRI. Having the x-ray and the ultrasound performed wasn't a big deal. But when Dr. Nichols started to explain the next steps to find the source of the problem with a MRI and if no answer we would then progress to a CT scan, I began to have some serious doubts that the problem had anything to do with my vertebrates. They wanted to look more in-depth into my muscles and other internal vital organs. The MRI result was then sent to a urology specialist to be examined. His examination revealed that there was a small spot underneath my left kidney. Within a couple days, I was having a CT scan performed to give a more definite answer. After the completion of the CT scan, an appointment was made for me to see a urology specialist, Dr. Carl Viviano, and he requested that I bring family. I knew what he had to share wasn't good news. So I took only my wife along with me to the appointment. I did not want my daughter and son there to hear what he had to say. I wanted to be the one to explain whatever the out-come of the CT scan was to them in my way and time. The CT scan revealed that the spot underneath my left kidney was indeed CANCER! The dreaded C word! And I needed to have the tumor removed.

God's mystery

God reveals Himself in strange methods and people to fulfill His healing promise. Now with the diagnosis of cancer, my back pains subsided but I was left to face a more serious dilemma. Quite naturally, facing the predic-ament of cancer placed a much more serious spin on life than facing back pains. I was now placed in a possible life-threatening dilemma; what was I to tell my daughter and son? Especially at this time, with all the emotion and anxiety centered on Lizzette's death and now her boy-friend had been charged with her murder. And the trial was set to start on Tuesday, July 5, 2005. If that wasn't enough, my wife fell the following week and broke a bone in her foot that required surgery. I began to con-template what message was in all of this or if there was a message at all from God. I knew a couple things for sure: I had cancer and nothing was going to stop me from being with my brother and his family during the murder trial. Dr. Viviano initially wanted to schedule the surgery for the end of April. With the trial set to begin in early July, I knew that it would be impossible for me to attend the trial while recovering from a major surgery. And with my wife needing foot surgery, she was unable to drive. So I opted to have the surgery done after the trial. I had to be there to share in the final closure to this whole scenario behind Lizzette's death. The trial lasted almost three weeks before a verdict came in on Friday, July 22, 2005. I had my surgery on the 28th of July, 2005.

The Trial

Sitting through Lizzette's murder trial was taxing enough, let alone traveling back to Wausau on two occa-sions to give blood at the blood bank for my upcoming surgery. I would sit through a four to six hour trial, then drive two and half hours home to Wausau and give a pint of blood on each occasion. After I had given blood, I would receive a cookie, some juice or a soda, and be instructed to stand up slowly to avoid dizziness. If no dizziness occurred, I was able to leave. If dizziness occurred, I had to wait at least a half hour or until my wooziness subsided before I would drive home or back to Madison for the next day's trial. The trial filled me and family members with great emotion and numbing pain. We sat and listened to the details surrounding Lizzette's murder including the forensic evidence collected from her apartment, her boyfriend's alibi at the time of Lizzette's death, what time he came home and found her and tried to revive her and the 911 calls he made! This emotional roller coaster trial ended with testimony from the prosecutor's expert witness that specialized in gunshot residue analysis that placed her boyfriend in their room with her at the time of the gunshot, as well as a very detailed cell phone history.

The Deliberation

On July 21, 2005, the case went to the jury after almost three weeks of testimony and closing arguments. The jury was still out after more than ten hours of deliberation. With the jury out all day Thursday and into that evening, some tension began to grow as to what the verdict might be. The longer the jury was out, the more I felt that the verdict would likely be innocent or a hung jury. Around ten o'clock p.m., the clerk of the court came out and told everyone to go home. Deliberation would recommence at nine o'clock on Friday morning, July 22, 2005. Would this be the date that our long wait would end and justice be served? That Friday morning was one of many prayers and supplications for justice for Lizzette. A few hours later, the jury returned with their verdict.

Immediately after the Judge read the verdict of "guilty," jubilation rang out in the courtroom as Lizzette's parents and many other family members sat trembling in their seats while clinging on to each other's hands and arms. I thought to myself we had gotten justice for Lizzette as we all wept, hugged and supported each other in the hallway outside the courtroom. Closure had finally come after years of agonizing over the traumatic death that had placed our family in such piercing pain of disbelief and heartache that would continue to haunt not only me but our entire family for years to come.

One painful hurdle behind

With that painful trial behind us, I still had to face another one, beating cancer. The next step in my fight against cancer was to prepare for the surgery. I had faith it would be successful. The procedure called for removing parts of the left kidney until all the cancer was gone. Approximately 8:00 a.m. the morning of my surgery, I was outside working in my garden as usual. My neighbors, Dr. Pablo Amador and his wife, Araceli, approached me and asked if my surgery appointment had been canceled or was I okay, with this discerning look on their faces and worry in their eyes, as if I was crazy to be outside working in my garden the morning of a major surgery. I said no, my surgery wasn't canceled. It was not until 11:00 a.m. and I needed to be at the hospital one hour before for prep. My state of mind wasn't to worry but to relax and trust God, and one of the best ways for me to relax was working in my garden. If I hadn't been working in my garden in the first place this blessing of discovery would not have happened.

The surgery was a success, and as of this writing the cancer has not returned. I also learned a vital lesson not only from the surgery but with life's adversities; how God works and moves in my life, leading me through life's trials and tribulations to healing. For me the surgery was like evil desires had been cut out of me. I cannot say for sure if I was dreaming after the surgery, or was it during surgery, or the medication that caused visions of headless men to appear before me. One thing I know for sure is that God is real and so is Christ. God can do just what His word says He can do. He healed me by communicating through strong Christians that I needed to bear my cross and have the surgery. I had been looking to be healed supernaturally without bearing my cross.

In evil's attempt to take my life with a slow-moving, hidden approach! It was defeated by God's blessing of an excruciating back pain that brought me back from a slow death sentence to one of triumph. Igniting a true blessing in disguise for me and my family that would propel me to hunt for my spiritual destiny in life.

Chapter 22

LOYALTY TO WHOM...

Matthew 6:24: "No one can serve two Masters..."

"For either he will hate one and love the other, or else he will be loyal to the one and despise the other. You cannot serve God and mammon." What I had failed to realize in my continuous pursuit of pinnacle destiny was what God's will was for my life. I continued to pursue it through my own strength, not realizing it at the time that there are two pinnacles in life: worldly and spiritual. Therefore, I asked myself this question: "Which one had enabled me to endure elementary school, with very grim hopes for completion, followed by the determination to graduate high school?" I had an infrequent acquaintance with our formal education system throughout my elementary and junior high school years, and that, coupled with my learning disabilities, made it difficult to keep the faith. Therefore, my high school graduation was just another achievement in life to reach my worldly status. Wrong! Apparently *"Nobody – Hey, Water Boy"* had it in him to conquer other continuing academic challenges to graduate college and work as an educational entrepreneur; was that my final standing?

The next question I asked myself was, "since I have already achieved a college degree and become an educational entrepreneur, is that good enough?" If not, then did I need to *obtain a Master's Degree and anything beyond?* Finally with a Master's in hand at the age of 62, I asked myself, was there a spiritual pinnacle status, and could I have both a worldly and spiritual status at the same time? Or would this be similar to trying to serve two masters at the same time; and I know what God's word says about that!

As you probably can tell by now that I wanted my accolades in life to come from worldly. Similarly to a Boys and Girls Club CEO by the way of FAM since my dream of NBA stardom was long gone. I wanted that beautiful brick home like the plantation owners, as I used to think about when I was Mom's helper and performed yard boy duties. I had been a loving and helping son, a good person, a hard worker, and most of all I *believed in* God and Christ. Therefore, where was my success in life? I guess you can say that I had been waylaid by the most important thing in order to achieve life's fame. Not realizing it I had become a person who was totally relying on his own abilities and strength to attain greatness. This deception landed me into a financial whirlwind of turmoil, and I was literally fighting for mine and FAM's existence each day.

Economically, things had gotten so bad that in June 2007 I had to remove myself from FAM's payroll as its paid owner and executive director and become its volunteer consultant. I became the director of educational materials with FAM's largest contributor and beloved friend, Bob Weirauch's company, Safe Assured Community Solutions, "SACS" program, to keep mine and FAM's family afloat. Bob-*say it ain't so Joe*-told me that "God had placed me with him for a short period of time and that God had bigger and better things planned for me in the future." It was so refreshing to hear such an admired and generous man speak so highly of God and me in the same voice. Even with God placing me in SACS, I knew that I would only be with that program for a short period of time, two or three years, due to the economy and other logistical factors. And if or when a change would come, I would be the first to go, since I was the last to be employed. When that change did come after a year and six months, I thank God that I was wrong and wasn't the first one to go.

Was it an honest mistake or profiling?

March 20, 2008, after one and half years of working in the WASD and seven years as FAM's founder and Executive Director, just weeks before I was to receive one of the first Marathon County's American Red Cross "Real Hero Award" for my outstanding contribution in working with the adolescents in the WASD through the FAM program. My son and I were leaving our house at approximately 7:30 pm to go to his tennis practice. He was dressed in his school tennis apparel and we were both wearing hoodies (his was red and mine black) with the logo across the front. As we walked out of our front door and down the driveway to Marsh's car that was parked in front of our house on our side of the street, I saw what I thought was a Wausau police car approaching from Grand Avenue. I later learned that it was actually a Wisconsin State Patrol car that had turned onto Kent Street, a half block away, driving slowly in our direction. By the time we reached the end of our driveway, so had the officer's car. He pulled over on his side of the street, rolled down his window and asked if he could talk with us. And I said yes, thinking that he might have recognized my son or me and wanted to speak with us about tennis or FAM. But to the contrary he asked where we were coming from and said we had to go with him because someone fitting my **description** had robbed a check cashing store a block away on Grand Avenue. I tried to explain to the officer that I had been home all evening and we were going to my son's tennis practice match and my wife was in the house and could witness for me. But he wouldn't listen to anything I had to say and insisted that we had to go with him to the crime scene to be identified, or not, by the manager of the check cashing store. Again, I tried to appeal to the officer that I had not robbed anyone and that we needed to get to my son's tennis game. There we were standing in front of our house and Marsh had his tennis bag on his shoulder trying to explain to this officer who we were. He never asked for any identification, only insisted that we had to go with him. I saw that we weren't getting anywhere in convincing him that we lived in the house where he saw us coming out of the driveway so I asked if we could at least drive to this place that I had allegedly robbed and he said yes.

We then got into Marsh's car and the officer followed behind us. The check cashing store was across Grand

Avenue from the Channel 9 ABC affiliate station and they had their cameras running as cars were passing by slowly looking at us. We were on display for all to see on one of the busiest streets in Wausau. To my astonishment, there were a total of six or eight Wausau police officers and a couple of detectives just standing around watching me as another detective was talking to the store manager. After about ten minutes had passed, one of the officers asked if he could search my son's car and his tennis bags, I said yes. So after about fifteen minutes of this profiling, I began to get irritated with the whole situation, mainly because several of those officers knew me from FAM and the Real Hero award promotion that had been on TV for several weeks and not one of them said anything on my behalf. I made no secret of how annoyed I was, and Marsh started to get very concerned that I was going to be arrested or accosted and told me to relax, that tennis practice wasn't important. Twenty minutes into that nightmare, the detective who was interviewing the store manager finally came over to me and for the first time we were asked us for some identification. Then he told us we could go and he knew where we lived if he needed us.

As we pulled away en route to the tennis center, an officer proceeded to follow us the entire way and watched us walk into the center. Marsh was very upset and his practice match went poorly. We later found out that the description of the alleged robber was a black male, about 5 feet 9 inches and in his mid-thirties. At the time, Marsh was in high school and I was 60 years old and we are both 6 feet 4 inches tall! About a week later, we did receive a gracious apology from the Wausau Chief of Police, and although a copy was sent to the State Patrol we received no acknowledgement.

That was the beginning of the end of me wanting to call Wausau my home. When I talked to Bob he told me "not to drive a moving truck up to my door to move based on that incident, but if I wanted to leave Wausau do so because of a better life." He was right.

Other accolades or blessings

On April 3, 2008, at an elegant award banquet, I received my Marathon County, Wisconsin, American Red Cross Real Heroes award for being a community hero to youth. This award was given to me for being an advocate for youth. For more than thirty-five years, I counseled, mentored and worked to protect young people, particularly those at risk. It was a humbling experience to receive such a prestigious award for doing what I loved, helping adolescents improve their lives both scholastically and personally. However, once I had received such esteemed recognition, I realized this was God's way of keeping me on the right path, because such an honorable recognition as a community hero carried great responsibilities. I had now been placed in the public eye with a task that was greater than just counseling, mentoring and protecting young people. Now I was a champion to them, too. This called for me to display godlikeness in everything I did and not revert back to my old ways of self-fulfillment and pride.

My employment with the SACS program gave me the opportunity to return to the University of Wisconsin–Stevens Point (UWSP) and complete my master's degree.

My anticipated return to grad school was filled with happiness as I was fired up to take on this challenge again. I enrolled in the winter semester 2008-09 and took evening classes so I could remain employed at SACS. However, with six years removed from the demanding academic pace required for graduate school made that initial happiness short lived (In the Fall of 1999, I had enrolled in UWSP but had to drop out for financial reasons). I was sixty years old when I returned to graduate school and sixty-two years old when I graduated. I experienced great difficulties in readjusting to the demanding work load and tempo that each class required. It took the entire first midterm to get acclimated again to the fast paced commitments to studying for grad school classes' preparation. This rekindled my late elementary and early junior high school days' frustration of trying to keep up academically and being the oldest student in my classes. Especially after one of my professors openly, in class, made reference to me being the oldest in her class; even older than her. She would interrupt me mid-sentence with a comment, "Joe, that's not what we are talking about." Just like those teachers in elementary and junior high school. Even before I had a chance to fully explain or express my thoughts. Making it seem that my age caused or slowed down class discussion since I took the long way around to explain something. I think a proper response could have been to get to the point and not just cut me off or down in front of the class. Therefore, I had to dig deep down inside of my soul and find that same strength that helped to propel me through tough academic times in Mississippi and Aurora College.

Please don't take this the wrong way because I didn't. For me it was just another motivational tool to help me prove that even being the elderly statesman student and out of touch with the demanding requirements for present day grad school, I could and did meet the challenges needed for graduation. Giving up wasn't and still is not a part of who I am and what I was born to do. And if I employ the mentality of being a quitter, I should just go somewhere and lie down and die, because I would be quitting on myself, my family and most of all on what God has created me to be within the body of Christ! Therefore, if I had employed a defeatist attitude in the eyes of adversity, then I am not who God said I was or could be, more than a conqueror. So like my elementary and junior high school years, I stayed and took those embarrassing moments because that is all they were, moments! And I didn't let them define who I was, for I had so much more to offer than to let some insignificant incidents change what God had in store for me. Also from those embarrassing moments, I realized there was more to grad school than them. I also met and was taught by some of the most devoted and helpful professors anyone could ever hope to meet who shared their many gifts and compassion to teach and develop future leaders. I likewise had classmates who were more than willing to share their intellect one to one or in a group setting. And with the leadership of my grad committee and a commitment to persevere, I was able to graduate May 21, 2010 with a Master of Science in Human and Community Resources.

Even after receiving my master's degree, I knew I would inevitably descend into the ranks of unemployment! When I did fall into the ranks of unemployment, surviving felt like a person who could not swim, attempting to swim upstream in a raging rapids with all the hardships of being jobless strapped to his back, especially for someone who never learned to swim. My initial thought of being without a job placed me in a frightful state of mind of being unable to support my family. What was I to do to make it through this unavoidable time in my life that could possibly drag me and my family into poorness? So I asked myself this question: am I going to let the ranks of unemployment be my EARTHLY PEAK status in life? If so, what a price to pay for all my hard work dating back to those horrible days in Mississippi, to possibly die in mediocrity in Wausau, Wisconsin. However, to make ends meet, I had to retire and file for my Social Security benefits to have that additional income coming in. I didn't know at the time that my employment with the SACS program, even though it was for a short period of time, would turn out to be a blessing in disguise. My benefits were being paid based on my last employment which was with the SACS program. This increased my benefits twice as much as if I had still been employed with FAM; thank God for placing me with SACS! Even though things weren't anywhere near what I pictured my apex to be, we were still blessed to have the income, and I did have to help pay the bills.

A Message or not!

In my humble opinion, some days were much more striking than others, filled with peace and tranquility. God's gorgeous blue sky was filled with stunning white fluffy clouds floating across it like sweet dreams I once knew in Mississippi. But then there were those days I compared as bad ones! The ones that transformed into the rainy days that said, "stay indoors and sleep." Subsequently some of those rainy days included dark nightmarish clouds as they overflowed with not only rain but thunder, lighting and fierce winds. Like I once overflowed with fears and risked disgrace to fulfill the cravings of my gloomy days. Therefore, to defeat my fears, which is opposite of faith, I turned to His word for all my protections and do not tempt God anymore. And be thankful that I have the freedom to openly seek and pray to Him each day; the opportunity is there for my life and my family's life.

While waiting for an answer to my petitions, I noticed for the first time several squirrels and chipmunks that seemed to be playing some kind of a game. So I asked myself what were they accomplishing with all their running and jumping around on those tree branches and utility wires, as they chased each other to what seemed like a no end result. This little voice inside of me said, "possibly it was the Holy Spirit; just watch and learn." Not only did this make me realize and see more of God's astonishing creation of life in those squirrels and chipmunks as they chased each other, I also saw all kinds of birds soaring and landing on the garage, cable and utility wires, and this display by them began to truly pique my curiosity about how God takes care of them. But this one bird in particular, a Dove, wasn't at all like the other birds that appeared to be playing a game as they soared and landed as they pleased. The Dove seemed to be carrying some kind of message to me by the way she would sit on the front top edge of my garage in the same spot each morning for weeks, for long periods of times facing in my direction. It seemed as though this Dove was looking at me as was I at her. Then there were days when she would sit looking in the other direction, and I assumed there was a reason or a message behind that, too. This might sound a little crazy or weird to some of you, or possibly to all of you, that this Dove was delivering to me some kind of message from God. Nonetheless, on those mornings that she would sit facing me, my thought came more clearly and precisely than on the days when she would sit with her back to me or wasn't there at all. The Book of Job 12:7-8 it says, *"now ask the beasts, and they will teach you; and the Birds of the air, and they will tell you; and the fish of the sea will explain to you."*

I have heard and know of people who used this phrase: "God works and sends messages in mysterious ways using various objects and things." The phrase "God works in mysterious ways" is not found word-for-word; in fact the word "mysterious" doesn't appear in the King James Bible or my student study Bible at all. This popular saying is possibly a paraphrase based on verses that spoke of God's "kingdom mystery;" for example, *Ecclesiastes 11:5: "As you do not know what is the way of the wind, Or how the bones grow in the womb of her who is with child, So you do not know the works of God who makes everything."* So was the **mystery** behind this Dove some kind of message or signal that says do not waver like the squirrels and chipmunks but have faith! And decide! Above all, do not swear either by heaven or by earth or with any other oath. *"But let your 'Yes' be 'Yes,' and your 'No,' be 'No' lest you fall into judgment,"* James 5:12.

I surely have been a branch hopper myself, bouncing around or faltering with my faith. Unfaithfully, I jumped from one thing to another in my pinnacle hunt– careers and relationships. I ask myself whom had I become? And one day as I looked into a mirror and didn't like what I saw, and I asked myself this question: "where have my loyalties gone?" As far as I can reflect back, it seemed like all of God's creatures had experienced some difficulty in choosing which path or nature to follow, even Adam and Eve, my fore parents. My free will has placed great difficulty in my ability to choose. I have learned that with free will, when it comes to dealing with life's fears, it is almost impossible to find completeness and comfort without God first. Does this sound like it's time to decide and only fear God and leave idolatry alone? God is joy through faithfulness of prayers; belief, tiding, and most importantly, love. I was so caught up in achieving greatness that it short circuited my loyalty to my God, nor was I thankful enough for what I already had or didn't remember that spiritual delusion was not for me since it **must depend on a specific status in life,** but God's Agape love doesn't!

Chapter 23

THE FINAL ACT OF WAUSAU...

In early February of 2011, Jean and I began to seriously doubt that I would find another job in Wausau. At this crossroad in our life, we began to strongly consider making a move to North Carolina if no job opportunity opened up for her in her employer's home office of Boston, Massachusetts. So we set a target date of March 1, 2011, to put our moving plan in motion by placing our home on the market, thinking it would take at least two or three months to sell it. This way we could still be in Wausau just an hour and half from our daughter, Nicci, to support her and her husband, Justin, with the birth of their first child and our first grandchild on March 3, 2011 and extend that support to them another two months or so before moving to North Carolina in late April or early May. Jean's younger sister, Julie, and her husband, David, and family (Carissa, Kendra and Ray) lived in North Carolina, and our son Marsh was in school in Wilmington, North Carolina; we thought that state was destined to be our next home.

Fear had now tried to become my worst enemy, and I could imagine what was going through my beloved Jean's mind. With us once again by faith picking up and moving not only to another state but this time cross country. Not knowing how quickly we could secure employment, or **if** we couldn't secure employment, we were determined to leave Wausau for a better job opportunity for both of us. We employed a close friend, Joe Landowski, who is a real estate broker to do an appraisal of our home to see how much equity we had. Now the stage was set for the final act in Wausau.

As faith would have it, Jean and I were already doing the will of God by preparing our home to go on the market for the best price possible. God had already put a plan in motion for us to move to Boston and not to North Carolina. God had had us start our home improvement preparation that previous summer with various small home improvement projects in preparation for my Master's graduation party in May of 2010. We as mortal human beings couldn't see into the invisible rim where our futures were being planned by God. The only thing we could do was to be patient and trust in Him to guide us.

Jean had been applying for a couple of jobs in Boston and neither one had panned out for her. She had received a phone call from the Boston office on Wednesday, February 19, 2011, asking her if she was still interested in moving to Boston and she said yes! But there were no offers made at that time. We thought if things did work out for us to move to Boston, it probably wouldn't happen in 2011. So we continued to prepare to move to North Carolina just in case. From this experience of preparing for a move with God in control, I learned a vital lesson. You must always be prepared because when God is in control, things happen in His timetable and not our timetable. As Mom always said, "He might not come when we want Him to but He is always on time." Therefore! Please be prepared. Since God does not reveal His personal timeframe for things to happen in life, I still count on Him to reveal things to me through His Word that can and does brings about life-changing occurrences. Miracles!

Ironically, when I in my early teens I thought that New England was a city of England and had vowed to live there one day. It always fascinated me to live in another country, and the way that people spoke of it I was sure it would be better than Mississippi. The way that I found out it was a part of the United States was because of a newspaper article that explained how a mother in New England had killed her daughter to keep her from running away with a black man. That deterred me from considering ever wanting to live there again. However, when I was little older I came to respect the Boston Celtics because of John Havlick, Bill Russell, and later when Dennis Johnson played. So luckily I stopped fearing New England; knowledge is power!

Friday! February 21, 2011, just a few days later, we found out that Liberty Mutual Insurance home office in Boston was definitely going to be Jean's next place of employment. After months of uncertainty, we now had just one month to sell our home in Wausau and find a place preferably southeast of Boston to live. Within a week, Jean had been relocated to the Boston office and was living in an upscale apartment in Boston's Back Bay Area a few blocks from work. In the meantime, I remained in Wausau to handle that end of our move. Things had begun to happen so fast that I barely had time to think. There were real estate brokers and agents; bank lenders and mortgage companies; the packing and moving company constantly calling almost daily. My email inbox was flooded with emails detailing who had the best lending rates and things to do from the relocation company that coordinated our move to the Massachusetts area.

Except for occasional short trips for business or to visit relatives and friends, we were separated now for the first time for more than a month in our twenty-one years of marriage. Also, this would be the first time Jean and I would be apart from each other on Valentine's Day; no big deal right? But the way things began to unfold with me joining her in Boston, uncertainty began to put doubts in my mind if this move was from God or had we made the right decision to move to the Boston area. Those doubts intensified even more when my first house-hunting trip to Boston had to be canceled due to a huge snow storm. I was scheduled to fly to Boston on Friday February 25 in the morning so we could start our house hunting that Friday afternoon and that following Wednesday. We had looked at houses online prior to Jean leaving for Boston, and our real estate broker had lined up houses for us to see, as well. To say the least, I didn't arrive in Boston until after midnight on Saturday. My Friday morning flight out of Wausau to Minneapolis was canceled due to that large snow storm gridlocking any incoming and outgoing flights to Minneapolis. I was then left with only one option, to be rerouted through Detroit late that Saturday evening and arrive in Boston at midnight.

Therefore, I didn't get a chance to tour the houses we had scheduled to view that Friday. With time running out for us to find a house, our Wednesday house hunt became imperative. This urgency to find houses in our price range southeast of Boston landed us in the towns of Bridgewater and East Bridgewater with the help of a friend, Paula. We looked at many houses in our price range between the two towns. And chose a lovely Deck home in the town of Bridgewater that needed some serious TLC. It had been unoccupied and on the market for two years. We had already accepted an offer on our home in Wausau and set a closing date for March 23 and we had to be out by midnight of the 24th of March, Jean's birthday. With time running out in our house hunt, we put in an offer that was close enough to their asking price and hard for them to refuse, so we were able set that closing date for March 30, 2011.

Now things seemed to be falling into place on both ends and that temporarily relieved some of my uncertainties about moving to the Boston area. But they were short lived since the buyer of our Wausau home knew that she had the upper hand with our need to sell quickly and started to take advantage of our situation to sell quickly. She asked us to pay for the closing cost; thousands of dollars toward replacing the furnace that the home inspector had said was in good working condition. Even after we agreed to sell the house for six thousand dollars below the listing price and took out a home warranty policy that would pay half the cost on anything that broke within a year of purchase.

To top that off the day of the closing, March 23, was the day the moving company was coming; I awakened to nine inches of new snow and I had sold my snow blower since it was too small for our new home's driveway. There I was snowed in with no snow blower and the movers waiting in their cars in front of the house for the moving truck to arrive. Then I saw what Mother Nature had left for me in the front of the house, too! Not to mention what the city snowplow driver had deposited for me at the end of the driveway. To my surprise, when I went to open the back door, the snow drifts had wedged it closed, and after I had forced it open to walk outside onto its stoop, I saw snow drifts that seemed to be almost four feet in height between the back steps to the front of the garage. In my panic-stricken state, I tried to figure out how I was going to shovel all that snow by hand before the moving truck arrived. In my attempt to get to the garage through the snowdrifts where I keep my snow SHOVEL was less of a struggle than dealing with the cool wind that sent bone-chilling feeling throughout my entire body. As I shoveled my way out of the garage to the back stoop and began to work my way down the driveway toward the front of the house my attempt was unsuccessful. That bone chilling wind keep blowing so hard that it was propelling the snow I had already shoved back over any progress I was making. As usual when I am in a tight spot and about to give up, God sends a helper, *just in time*. This time it was our next door neighbor, Dr. Amador's handyman who came to my rescue. He plowed the driveway from the street to the garage and the sidewalk, minutes before the moving truck arrived.

The remainder of that day was filled with shadowing the driver as he listed, labeled and tagged every box, piece of furniture and any other items in the house, basement and garage. I also made sure that the driveway and walkway to the front stoop stayed as clean as possible of snow for the guys who were loading the van line. What proficiency they displayed in loading all the boxes, items and furniture room by room and the garage. This was an all-day process, and at the end of the day, I was overwhelmed as the driver and I made the final sweep throughout the house and garage. As I packed my overnight luggage and walked out of 127 Kent Street at approximately 5:00 pm for the last time it felt very strange, and I was overcome with both joy and sadness seeing the house totally empty for the first time since we moved there ten and half years earlier. Our cars had been taken the day before by a transport company to the home of our real estate broker in Bridgewater. That night I stayed in a hotel and used a loaner car from our dearest friends Rand and Kerrie Huebner, who also would take me to the airport in Milwaukee the next morning to fly to Boston. Realizing that I had spent my last night in the house where I and Jean had experienced both hard times and good times was almost overwhelming. We shared our home, love and hospitality of fellowshipping with family members, friends, neighbors and care groups from church. But the love and joy of seeing our beloved children, Nicci and Marsh, grow into young adulthood in that house and then venture out on their own overshadowed them all. To me there was something really very special about our Wausau home. It seemed to bring out the best in each one of us, and to this day I still refer to it as God's house. He just loaned it to us for ten and half years.

How Great is God!

Philippians 4:13: *...all things are possible through Christ who strengthens me*

Within a week God, had relocated Jean to Boston. Six weeks later, we were living in a lovely Deck home in the town of Bridgewater, Massachusetts, to embark upon another chapter in our life. I believe this had been planned out for Jean and me by God through our Lord and Savior Jesus Christ even before we were born; me to a Mississippian sharecropper, and her to a Wisconsin disc jockey and nurse. So I must honestly say that at the present time I am still waiting to see—funny words, To SEE (especially since the mystery of my Savor's Kingdom is not to SEE but to *live by faith and not by sight, II Corinthians 5:7*) where His Beyond will take me next. All I know is that I must follow where He leads me. And if this is His Beyond or pinnacle status for me, I will wait patiently for it to materialize.

Coming from a background such as I did, initially I found the Town of Bridgewater to be quiet and somewhat *dreamlike* or surreal. God has surrounded me with three wonderful neighbors to learn from, especially Jose (Joe) Pimentel and his wife, Marie; and the Ghelfiand's (Albert "Abby" and Gail); and Thrasher's (Keith and Doris); and we all share many similarities: a strong commitment to family values; a sense of community and the willingness to help each other; respect; and we have wonderful wives! There are many other positive things I have learned from my neighbor Joe: everything is done in its own time frame; willingness to share the products of a garden harvest; craftsmanship gifts and talents that go "beyond" just giving and being a helpful neighbor, including being there with me until the jobs are finished, constantly teaching and having patience. Even God rested on the Sabbath day. For *me* –Now! I have finally begun to really understand the *total* essence of what it takes to live God's rewarding life. With God in control of my life, there isn't anything that cannot be accomplished.

"Be anxious for nothing"

Three years have passed since we relocated to Bridgewater and I'm still waiting for God, through Christ, to disclose my Beyond. However, God has continued to reveal Himself to me of how important it is to have faith in good times as well as in bad. If I don't continue to place myself, love ones, cares, concerns, and hopes with patience or questions about why evil and senseless acts happen and try to destroy or takeaway that *Faith* so desperately needed for survival. Then who can I turn to in my time of need. That's why He gave us His "Word" to rely upon! Jesus Christ! As stated in Philippians 4:6, *"Be anxious for nothing, but in everything by prayer and supplication, with Thanksgiving let your request be known to God!"*

Still believing that God has a destiny for me that is comprised of great prosperity, given that I continue to be retired, we rarely shop for pleasure, but on April 14, 2013 we decided to put aside our anxiety and take a day for ourselves. It was Patriots Day, the running of the Boston Marathon, which meant it was a holiday for my wife. We decided to take advantage of her day off work and took a trip to an outlet mall in Wrentham, hoping that parking and shopping wouldn't be so chaotic with the running of the Marathon. It turned out be to a relaxing day at the mall, and the next stop on that day's schedule was the grocery store. We were near completion of our grocery shopping when my wife received a phone call from her brother, Jim, asking if we were okay. He had seen the bombing on television and knew it was near or at the Marathon finish line just two blocks from Jean's work. In shock and disbelief that such an event could have taken place, we rushed to finish shopping and headed home to see what was on local news about the bombing. To our surprise, it was a devastating and heart-wrenching real event. We watched the whole scene play out that afternoon and into the late evening. Admittedly, our prayers and supplications were with everyone who was affected by that hideous act, the victims and the first responders (professional to the non-professional), families, friends and even the perpetrator of that repulsive violent and evil act.

As we sat and watched one miracle after another unfold from that absurd act of evil against a **soft shell** event of so many innocent runners, loved ones, family members, friends, and bystanders reinforced everything that I had written thus far and believe about what a wonderful God that I serve. Because no matter what your cross to bear is, He will never leave or forsake you. He is always with you.

I did not personally know anyone that ran in the marathon but Jean had a coworker that was running, it hit home for us. We had made countless visits to Boylston Street, the Commons, Copley Square and surrounding community; sightseeing with family members, friends and just being tourists. My wife's work is just a couple of blocks from the finish line. Besides that, when we first relocated we lived in the Boston historic Back Bay area for a couple of months before moving to Bridgewater. Jean made craft flowers that she placed at one of the memorials that developed near the bombing sites. She talked of the eeriness of going back to work when the streets surrounding the site, including directly outside the office doors, were closed and seeing all of the bags flying around the empty streets that were left by the runners. Then again throughout the week, we were glued to the television, watching everything unfold. Jean had to work in New Hampshire on the day the city was locked down. It was all so implausible.

Over the last year, I have learned what it really means to be a New Englander. That passion of togetherness has built a stronger bond of inseparability of all for one and one for all. A never-ending array of hope, miracles and an outpouring of support all aided by those prayers and supplications from around the world. What a joy to see as so many people laid aside their own personal agenda for one shared cause, a way of life that fear, wickedness and violence will not end. The Boston Marathon, Boston Strong!

Chapter 24

I'M SOMEBODY!

It was letting God's will in my life that transformed me into Somebody from that Nobody through His salvation of everlasting grace of a blessed peace of mind, joy and love, not money. Please don't get me wrong, I am not saying nor did God say that we shouldn't have prosperity in life to enjoy the good things He has for us. Money cannot buy the most vital things in life: true friendship, peace, joy, patience, goodness, happiness, or produce that Agape love of eternal life. Therefore, I have learned that if I invest what God has given me positively and righteously for the betterment of His kingdom, He will give me more. As displayed in the parable that Jesus taught on the talents in *Matthew 25:15*.

This shouldn't be a hard choice, *right,* if you look at it through life's realities that places two roads or choices before you to follow or travel. I had to realize that everything I owned or lost from sowing in unfruitful soil belonged to God. And I needed to make a conscious decision to start believing and accepting God's word to remove all the turmoil from my life before I could see the light of redemption. In making my final transformation from Nobody to Somebody, I had to accept and live my life in accordance with God's word. Now as Somebody through faith and believing *IN* God not just believing there is a God.

One way I determined whether or not I was still pre-occupied with self-gratification was to review my reasons behind the pursuit of it. If my hunt for pinnacle status was for God's kingdom and I was obedient to His command-ments, that's good. That's obedience to God. Otherwise, if my hunt was that I wanted to become successful in life so that I could help others to grow spiritually, that would be ok, too. That's Agape love. But if my hunt was solely to accumulate wealth for my selfish needs and social prominence, that's bad! That's Vanity. As I have stated throughout this narrative, at one time this was the case. So the final compelling question becomes, Can I refrain from Striving for worldly fame? And continue as God's Somebody!

Each day in God's kingdom is a new day filled with opportunities for me and anyone else if they so desire to grow their faith to please God and become fishermen of mankind for His Kingdom!

Ecclesiastes 3:1-8 Everything Has Its Time...
To everything there is a season,
A time for every purpose under heaven:
A time to be born,
And a time to die;
A time to plan,
And a time to pluck what is planted;

A time to kill,
And a time to heal;
A time to breakdown,
A time to build up;
A time to weep,
And a time to laugh;
A time to mourn,
And a time to dance;
A time to cast away stones,
A time to gather stones;
A time to embrace,
A time to refrain from embracing;
A time to gain,
A time to lose;
A time to keep,
A time to throw away;
A time to tear,
And a time to sew;
A time to keep silence,
A time to speak;
A time to love,
And a time to hate;
A time for war,
And a time for peace.

Chapter 25

REFLECTIONS

Philippians 4:19: *"But my God shall supply all your need, according to His riches in glory by Christ Jesus"*

With Christ, we can have joy in all things… As a final reflection, I will pull back from my passion for the Lord and reflect on my history and how it affected my life, and subsequently, my wife and children. I literally drank out of water fountains for "coloreds only," used "coloreds only" restrooms and couldn't go to the local small movie theatre until it was a deprived hand-me-down for "coloreds only." I know that everyone is a part of some living history. I have been privileged to give talks on Dr. Martin Luther King Jr. holiday to students at a technical college, on Wisconsin Public Radio, as well as to the many youth that I have worked with over the past few decades. Most couldn't imagine that I lived in a time when there was racial segregation. I lived the history that was never taught to me in school as most are today, which puts a whole different perspective on my life.

Having lived in the Midwest for many years, I find it strange that growing up I was a sharecropper and never labeled a farmer, as I would have been had I grown up in this area. It shows the stigma that is tied back to ownership and all that implies. I am not unhappy, by any stretch of the imagination, that I grew up the way I did. I was raised by strong women and a deep-seated faith in Jesus Christ. I have coping skills that others will never have related to life and surviving social injustices. How many people grew up like I did and see interracial families as a norm? As little as 10 years ago when we were visiting a black friend in Jackson, Mississippi, his daughter was a bit confused. She stated directly to my wife, "You're white and your husband is black?" Not the social norm for her; it didn't make sense to her. As a family, we are proud to help break down these old racial stigmas. We taught our children that it is the other people's problem, not theirs, if others have an issue with them or their heritage. My children have a strong Midwestern accent and that sometimes confuses people as well. Many assume they should speak in a stereotypical Ebonics-type dialect. In fact, my son was in a high school play, Rowan and Martin's Laugh-In, and was playing "The Judge" and the director asked if Marsh could speak a little more urban!

You would think that being married in 1989 that our interracial marriage would not have been that unique — hadn't society come a long way? — but Jean and I have been through many trials, often subtle. And some not so subtle: in Monona (suburb of Madison) we were denied housing; we were waiting outside a house that we were interested in renting and the owner simply drove right by and did not keep the appointment. When we moved to Wausau, it was particularly noticeable. We were watched wherever we went, at school, the mall, grocery stores, department stores and even church. The first church we visited, no one welcomed us and the preacher walked the other way and didn't greet us after service. When we were in a K-mart, a gentlemen was staring to the point that he walked into a display case. While operating FAM, some school personnel and teachers would go behind my back and talk to my staff who were white and Asian rather than me. To prove a point to myself, I took my wife to an IEP (Individualized Educational Program) meeting as a board member, not a staff, and they directed all of their questions to her instead of me. Over the last three decades, even in my new subculture (retiree), I have been the only fly in the buttermilk, so to speak. Recently, I was in the grocery store to pick up few things and walking briskly through the aisle; I saw an item that I needed but wasn't on my list so I stopped abruptly to get it and noticed a guy following me. He had to stop abruptly, too, so it became very obvious what his intent was. Then I realized that he had followed me before. What an angry, sick and irritable feeling came over me that even in the twenty first century just because of the color of my skin and semi-casual attire I was being stalked like a common shoplifter. But like I tell my children, it is his problem not mine!

Both of our children experienced some issue at school, both obvious and subtle, as well, but I don't think that they give it much thought today, thus surpassing my generation in moving beyond the cognizant racial issues. People will always find differences to separate themselves into classes, whether it be race, religion, money, country, etc. During my history and my ancestors before me, it has been race, which seems to want to hold on.

We are truly and simply a family. Two adults, two children, a son-in-law and one grandchild (at this writing). No pets though—too many allergies. Because of my background we were in the category of overprotective parents. I used my unique counseling skills in the form of lectures to handle any problems with the kids; groundings were not necessary. They laugh about it now, but at the time it was pure torture! We love to get together with family and friends whenever we can and miss it greatly now that we are in Massachusetts. As a result of my history, I tend to be seen as a very serious or stern person, but in reality I am simply a reflection of my past. Once you get to know me, I do have a subtle and simple lifestyle, a kind heart, and I do have fun; especially playing tennis in nearby Lakeville, and of course, Go Bears…"Da Bears!"

Even though society has come a long way in my lifetime, there is so much more to do. My children will do more to improve the world than I ever will, and they are my proudest accomplishment since they know and have experienced that there is no situation too hopeless for God!

Chapter 26

SOME OF MY FAVORITE VERSES

The Value of a Friend

Ecclesiastes 4: 9-12 (paraphrase): "Two are better than one, because they have a good reward for their labor. For if they fall, one will lift up his companion. But woe to him who is alone when he falls, for he has on one help him up. Though one may be overpowered by another, two can withstand him and a threefold cord is not quickly broken." Clearly, the image of marriage came to mind when I read these verse. A husband and wife can face the challenges of this world system together. And with God makes up the three-fold-cord theory.

The Vanity of Gain and Honor

Ecclesiastes 6:10-15 (paraphrase): "He who loves silver or gold will not be satisfied with them. Nor he who loves wealth, will increase. This is vanity. But riches will perish by misfortune and when you create a son, there is nothing in his hand as he come from his mother's womb, naked shall he return, to go as he came into this world. He like you shall take nothing from his labor away in his hand."

Assurance of the Resurrection
II Corinthians 5:7: "For we walk by FAITH, not by sight."

Be United, Joyful, and in Prayer
Philippians 4:6: "Be anxious for nothing, but in everything by prayer and supplication, with thanksgiving, let your request be made known to God.

Simple Trust in the Lord
Psalm 131:1 "Lord, my heart is not haughty, nor my eyes lofty. Neither do I concern myself with great matters, nor with things too profound for me..."

Do the Will of God
1 John 2:17: "And the world is fading away, and the lust of it; but he who does the will of God abides forever."

Not Hard at All
1 John 5:3-4: "For this the Love of God, that we keep His commandments. And His commandments

are not burdensome (means doing what He tells us to do, and really that isn't hard at all; to defeat sin and evil pleasure by trusting Christ to help)."

Praise Brings Blessings

Psalm 100:4–5: "Enter into His gates with thanksgiving, and into His courts with praise. Be thankful to Him and bless His name. For the Lord is good; His mercy is everlasting, and His Truth, Jesus, endures to all generations."

DEFINITION OF TERMS:

The following terms should help clarify this book and the ethnographic research I used to support my autobiography:

- ➤ **Skeeter – Nobody**
- ➤ **Dandies**- Elegantly dressed land owners, men.
- ➤ **Slavery**–The practice of one individual or entity owning another.
- ➤ **Slave**–One owned and forced into service by another.
- ➤ **KKK** -Ku Klux Klan
- ➤ **Lynching**–Being put to death by hanging by an unruly mob.
- ➤ **Sharecropper**–A farmer who works another's land in return for a share (ha ha) of the crop.
- ➤ **Plantation** –An agricultural estate worked by resident laborers.
- ➤ **Anchor Curve**–A small, unincorporated village surrounded by cotton fields.
- ➤ **Water Boy**–One who carried water in a pail to those who worked the fields.

- ➤ **Slave Auction**–A place where people were sold as slaves to other people. In slave auctions, families were frequently split up and sold to different owners.
- ➤ **Slave Auctioneer**–One who calls out and sells property (in this case, SLAVES) to the highest bidder.
- ➤ **Negroes**–Slang for people of the black race. The word *Negro* means "black" in <u>Spanish</u> and <u>Portuguese</u>.
- ➤ **Black as ebony**– Meaning: as black as Ebony, a very dense blackwood.
- ➤ **Brown** – A biracial person.
- ➤ **Darkey**–A very dark person of African descent; **Yellow** – A lighter biracial person.

Abbreviated (shortened) school year! The end result of a practice that allows children more time to work in cotton fields and other farms during harvest times.

CPSIA information can be obtained at www.ICGtesting.com
Printed in the USA
BVOW11s1128040815

411614BV00004B/33/P